PARENT
PARTNERS

WORKSHOPS TO FOSTER

SCHOOL/HOME/FAMILY

PARTNERSHIPS

*A Guide to
Presenting
Parent Education
Workshops*

by
Jacqueline Barber *with*
Lynn Barakos *and* **Lincoln Bergman**

LHS GEMS

Great Explorations in Math and Science
Lawrence Hall of Science
University of California at Berkeley

Cover Design
Carol Bevilacqua

Illustrations
Patricia Lima

Photographs
Dan Krauss

Lawrence Hall of Science, University of California,
Berkeley, CA 94720-5200

Director: Ian Carmichael

©2000 by The Regents of the University of California.
All rights reserved. Printed in the United States of America.
Pages intended to be reproduced for workshop participants
during the activities may be duplicated for classroom and
workshop use. All other text may not be reproduced in any
form without the express written permission of the copyright
holder. For further information, please contact GEMS.

Printed on recycled paper with soy-based inks.

International Standard Book Number: 0-924886-54-4

COMMENTS WELCOME !

Great Explorations in Math and Science (GEMS) is a growing
resource for inquiry-based science and mathematics education. GEMS publications are revised periodically, to incorpo-
rate user comments and new approaches. We welcome your
criticisms, suggestions, helpful hints, and any anecdotes
about your experience presenting these parent education
activities. Please send your comments to: GEMS Revisions/
Parent Partners, c/o Lawrence Hall of Science, University of
California, Berkeley, CA 94720-5200. The phone number is
(510) 642-7771 and the fax number is (510) 643-0309. You can
also reach us by e-mail at gems@uclink4.berkeley.edu or visit
our web site at www.lhs.berkeley.edu/GEMS.

This guide is intended for educators or activist parents who, aware of the many benefits, want to increase the role of parents and other adult caregivers in their children's schooling and at home. The materials in this guide are designed for parents of elementary-grade students. While the focus is on science and mathematics education, many of the materials relate to education in general.

These GEMS parent education programs are sponsored in part by grants from the Hewlett Packard Company and the people at Chevron USA. GEMS and the Lawrence Hall of Science greatly appreciate this support.

Field Testers

The following is a list of those who assisted in the testing process for these GEMS parent education materials. The list combines those who presented and reviewed these materials in both the first and second stages of testing. We are deeply appreciative to all of these educators and parent advocates whose detailed feedback helped guide our revision process. Their participation does not necessarily imply endorsement of the GEMS program or of any opinions or views expressed in these materials. THANKS!

ALABAMA
Cathy Coleman, Chickasaw

ARIZONA
Brownie Lindner, Flagstaff

ARKANSAS
Charlcie Strange, Conway

CALIFORNIA
Rosemary Cruz, San Diego
Marlo Duffin, Torrence
Monika Ely, San Diego
Jan Gurnee, Modesto
Linda Koravos, San Diego
Laura Lowell, Walnut Creek
Lindy Mateas, Santa Clara
Lynn Moorhead, Mountain View
Dorothy Patzia, Redwood City
Anita Reid, Palo Alto
Becky Siino, Mountain View
Cheryl Tekawa-Pon, San Lorenzo
Chuck Untulis, Palo Alto
Caroline Yee, Oakland

COLORADO
Karen Hunter, Longmont
Scott Sala, Denver

FLORIDA
Carol Marino, Vero Beach

IDAHO
Karey Dahlgren, Hayden Lake
Nancy Stevenson, Hayden Lake

ILLINOIS
Brenda Cox, Loves Park

MASSACHUSETTS
Les Bemal, Chelmsford

MICHIGAN
Terry Parks, Port Huron

MINNESOTA
Laddie Elwell, Bemidji

MISSOURI
MaryJo Coughlin, Kansas City
Matt Maniaci, Glendale
Ellen Schroeder, St. Louis
Pat Windship, Jennings

NEVADA
Gail Bushey, Dayton

NEW HAMPSHIRE
Carol McKinney, Milford
Kathy Parker, Milford

NEW MEXICO
Maddie Ziegler, Albuquerque

NEW YORK
Paul Young, Buffalo

NORTH CAROLINA
Pat Bowers, Chapel Hill

NORTH DAKOTA
Julie Gronos, New Town

OHIO
Nancy Houston, Dayton

OKLAHOMA
Linda Atkinson, Norman
Leslie Williams, Norman

PENNSYLVANIA
Caroline Crew, Lansdale

RHODE ISLAND
Pat Dulac, East Greenwich

TENNESSEE
Barbara Fulmer, Chattanooga
Renee Polson, Surgoinsville

TEXAS
Terry Brandhorst, Seabrook
Tracy Friday, Colleyville
Karen Ostlund, Austin
Armida Ramirez, El Paso
Becky Stanford, Odessa
Cathy Whitlow, San Antonio

UTAH
Sally Ogilvie, Layton
David Rivers, Wendover

WASHINGTON
Debbie Brandt, Bellevue
Anne Kennedy, Vancouver
Susan Schnapp, Vancouver
Laura Tucker, Port Townsend

WEST VIRGINIA
Andrea Ambrose, Charleston

WISCONSIN
Michelle Weisrock, Milwaukee

Acknowledgments

There are many people who helped bring this new GEMS publication to life:

* The educators, teachers, and parents who expressed the need for including parents in the discussion of educational reform issues and encouraged us to develop the venue for doing this;

* The hundreds of parents from Harding and Madera Schools in El Cerrito, CA, and Jefferson School in Berkeley, CA, who participated in a needs assessment of what—as parents—they wanted to learn in relation to their children's academic success and how they wanted to learn about it;

* Jan Hustler, Lindy Mateas, and Lynn Morehead of the Bay Area Schools for Excellence in Education (BASEE) program, who provided early insightful feedback on the prototype parent sessions;

* The dozens of educators (and parents) who presented the Parent Partners programs to a wide diversity of parent audiences in many different locations (listed on the preceding page);

* The hundreds of parents (and teachers) who participated in pilot *Parent Partners* programs and gave us their candid and thoughtful feedback;

* Nancy Thomas of the Hewlett Packard Company who recognized the need for these materials and helped to promote their use throughout the significant network of Hewlett-Packard communities.

In each case, we are highly appreciative of the comments and ideas these parents and educators contributed which led to important changes and improvements in the materials. The eagerness to try out and review these materials also reinforced our sense that such programs will be needed and welcomed at schools and in communities around the country.

The authors would also like to thank the following Lawrence Hall of Science staff members for their dedicated and persistent participation in the development and refinement of the materials in this book: Kathy Barrett, Kevin Beals, Kimi Hosoume, Kathy Long, JohnMichael Seltzer, and Carolyn Willard.

Extra thanks to Patricia Lima for her inspired and friendly illustrations in all likelihood drawn with children afoot!

In addition, we would like to acknowledge the creators of the following bodies of work, each of which influenced the development of the *Parent Partners* materials:

* Dr. Michael H. Popkin and the Active Parenting group. Special thanks for permission to use portions of their outstanding book, *Helping Your Child Succeed in School: A Guide for Parents of 4 to 14 Year Olds*, by Michael H. Popkin, Bettie B. Youngs, and Jane M. Healy, available from Active Parenting Publishers, Atlanta, Georgia, 1995. We provide additional information on their other offerings, including many excellent videos, on page 64;

* The Lawrence Hall of Science EQUALS and Family Math programs and staff, past and present, who have enlightened many of us about the crucial role of parental and community involvement and the importance of achieving equity and full inclusion in education. Educators from the EQUALS and Family Math programs have long been in the forefront of efforts nationwide and internationally to place mathematics education on a new footing of equality, and to devise compelling and relevant cooperative problem-solving opportunites for students and families that illuminate many branches of mathematics. Family Math activites, published in book form by the Lawrence Hall of Science, are used very widely, at schools and community centers, throughout the United States and internationally. Through active participation in interesting and accessible workshops, Family Math helps the entire family transform their attitude and gain confidence in mathematics—a key gateway to many careers. We provide additional program and contact information on Family Math on page 64.

* The research of Laurence Steinberg, as reported in his book, *Beyond the Classroom: Why School Reform has Failed and What Parents Need To Do*;

* The work of the National Committee for Citizens in Education as shared in *A New Generation of Evidence: The Family is Critical to Student Achievement* edited by Anne T. Henderson and Nancy Berla.

On a more personal note, as we developed the *Parent Partners* program, all of the authors endeavored to interweave whatever wisdom we have gained from our own personal experiences with our professional expertise as educators. Therefore we acknowledge our parents, helpmates, and offspring: Emma Lou, Carl, Steve, Saul, Leib, and Jesse; John, Eva, Kevin, and James; and Anne, Leibel, Lisa, Gayle, Anna, and Caitlin.

Contents

Foreword

"The evidence is now beyond dispute. When schools work together with families to support learning, children tend to succeed not just in school, but throughout life..."

> —from the Introduction to *A New Generation of Evidence: The Family Is Critical to Student Achievement*, Anne T. Henderson and Nancy Berla, editors, Center for Law and Education, Washington, D.C., 1994

School policy and encouragement to involve parents and caregivers in their children's education is a relatively new phenomenon. Lack of authentic parent involvement has reinforced separation of school and home cultures for many children and fueled recent backlash reactions to new developments in curriculum and instruction. Parent involvement can be a powerful force for positive change, when it is founded on the basis of mutual respect and cooperative interaction between school and home.

Some of the first work with families in mathematics education that has been extensively disseminated built on the desire and interest of parents and caregivers to help their children with math at home. The EQUALS program at the Lawrence Hall of Science developed FAMILY MATH in 1981–82. We began the work of preparing leaders for family classes in 1983, drawing from teachers, parents, administrators, and community members.

FAMILY MATH classes provided families with hands-on problem-solving activities that reinforced the school curriculum and could be repeated at home. They demonstrated the rationale for reform measures, presented learning experiences for both adults and children, and were enjoyable. In addition, they also presented role models and career information that emphasized the importance of mathematics to future education and work. Up to that time, little work had been done to involve parents and caregivers in math or science with their children. There was also relatively little research on parent involvement at that point. Today there is a growing collection of new information and reports about these topics. FAMILY MATH continues to thrive and grow nationally and internationally, and there are many other excellent parent involvement and family education programs.

This new GEMS publication, *Parent Partners*, provides formal outlines for three meetings to share recent research and its implications with parents and caregivers, together with sessions that help explain the rationale for today's reforms in science and mathematics education and the more modern approach to testing and assessment of children's progress in these subjects. Extensive handouts and detailed outlines offer step-by-step organization and timing for the three sessions and allow efficient preparation for the leaders. Leaders do not have to ferret through the mass of current literature, originate their own presentations, and pick out activities that fit. References and resource lists provide both participants and leaders with many options for further learning.

The points made in each session address important issues that face families and schools as we enter this new century. Crucial information is presented in each meeting. Hands-on activities are designed to reinforce the information and informal discussions give parents and caregivers time to plan for the educational involvement they want to implement with their own families after the series.

When you prepare for your work with parents and caregivers, you will find this book a useful resource. It will provide you with materials to help involve more parents in your school community. As you get ready, be sure to reach out to all families in your school and community when you recruit for your sessions, not just those who are always there. Think about how best to attract those who are not usually in attendance, thus providing the opportunity to enhance and enlarge parent involvement in your setting.

by Virginia Thompson, Former Director, FAMILY MATH

Introduction

Brief Overview

This guide contains a set of tools to use in the education of parents and other caregivers. These include:

- Detailed, step-by-step instructions for the presentation of three parent education sessions. The session topics are:

    How Parents Make a Difference
    How Students Learn Best
    Testing: Knowing What Your Child Knows

- Take-home articles and handouts focused on concrete things parents can do.

- Short information digests to be used in the school bulletin to reach the larger community of parents who were not able to attend the presentations.

These will be explained in greater detail later in this introduction. All of these tools grew out of careful analysis of the extensive research on parental involvement and student academic success, combined with a needs assessment that included direct input from hundreds of parents, field tests with dozens of educators who in turn presented these sessions to hundreds more parents, and our own experience as both parents and science/mathematics educators.

Before providing you with suggestions for using these tools, we wanted to share the reasoning behind these GEMS parent education efforts and provide you with some information on the crucial role of parental involvement. In turn, this background should prove very helpful in responding to parent concerns and tailoring your own presentations. Please note later sections in this introduction on recruitment of parents and other important factors to consider in making the most effective use of this parent education program.

A Pressing Need for Parent Education

All one needs to do is chat with parents on the school playground before school to quickly discern the level of concern and doubt that parents feel about the current state of education. Will my child learn to read? To write well? To master mathematics? To do well on standardized tests? These concerns are reinforced by all we hear in the media about failing education. At the same time, in our work with teachers, we have noticed a striking increase in teacher frustration with parents. A veteran teacher, talking about how things have changed over the past couple of decades, spoke about how students haven't gotten harder—but working with parents has.

This gap in perception, confidence and communication eats away at the essential partnership between teachers and parents. **It prevents many students from having the benefit of their parents and their teachers working together as active partners—and that is the goal.** Overwhelmingly the research shows that best results happen (for students *and* for schools) when parents are involved and know what to do, and when teachers and parents respect and understand each other's roles.

Parents need to be educated about the value of key educational reforms and enlisted to serve as powerful advocates for their children and for schools. Until recently, parents have been largely excluded from the educational round table, and this shows in the lack of knowledge and information that they have about the rationale behind new teaching practices. Over the past decade, mathematics and science educators and policymakers have introduced educational innovations and major policy reforms. They have, for example, changed the definition of what it means to be scientifically literate; advocated new ways for student progress to be evaluated; changed the norm for what good science and mathematics education looks like; and modified teaching methods for the inclusion and success of all students. Parents are for the most part unaware of the rationale behind these educational changes, leading to confusion and concern when they observe that their children's schooling is different from their own. Parents often ask: What is the value of the new approaches to teaching science and mathematics? What was the problem with the way it used to be? How can I help my child succeed in math and science?

When parents do not understand current best practices and instructional goals, they may have a tendency to incorrectly evaluate what is happening at their child's school. Teachers are too often beleaguered by the steep demands of today's classroom—the thought of being responsible for educating 30 students *and* as many as 60 parents is exhausting. Yet the result of having parents who are suspicious of innovative instructional practices means having to respond to constant negative feedback. Further, uninformed parents and a misinformed public can fuel a societal backlash against inquiry-based instruction, authentic assessment, and other keystones of good science and mathematics instruction called for by national standards.

Activist parents can and do serve as a powerful force for constructive change in a school community. They can educate other parents and community members. They can serve as strategic public relations resources with school boards. They can provide appropriate external pressure to schools, or teachers within schools, to change. **To play these roles appropriately, parents need an opportunity to learn and understand the value of key educational reforms.**

Beyond the value of learning about current educational practices, there is a need to inform parents about the tremendous power they have in relation to their children's academic success. **There are decades of research studies that point to parent involvement in a child's education as the single most important factor for academic success—more important than a parent's own situation, background, or education.** It is probably safe to say that most parents aren't aware of this research and what it says. Many don't know what is meant by "parent involvement" or how they go about playing the role of an involved parent. This could be called one of the "best-kept secrets" in educational research—it needs to be known and understood much more widely.

The encouraging news is that "being involved" doesn't require knowledge of math or science, a college education, or any extensive preparation. Research has shown that there are a collection of concrete actions, many of them small, that together can make a huge difference for children. Thus, **a key feature of any parent education program must be to inform parents of their power and then to unleash that power through helping them know what they can do and how to do it. That is what these materials are designed to do.**

What Parents Want

In developing these materials, we consulted with several hundred parents of elementary-grade children in urban public schools about what they wanted to learn in relation to their children's math and science education and how they wanted to learn it. These strong messages emerged:

- Parents are more interested in *how* they can enable their child's success rather than the specifics of *what* their children know, don't know, or should know.

- Parents want to be addressed directly as adult learners, to learn from "experts" through information sessions designed for adults, through reading, and through discussion.

- Parents are willing to attend more than one session to learn how they can contribute to their child's success, but they are also interested in learning in a variety of other time-efficient and practical ways, including by reading short digests in the school bulletin or articles about the topic sent home with their child.

This input guided the development of the tools in this guide.

Subsequently, we field-tested these materials at sites nationwide. Dozens of educators used these tools with hundreds of parents. An interesting finding emerged: **what educators think parents should know and feel comfortable in presenting is not always what parents want to know and feel comfortable learning.** Specifically, given the reality of parents' time-pressured lives, they were impatient with situations in which they needed to actively discover things themselves through hands-on approaches. Instead, **parents are hungry for information and a chance to think about how they could apply that information in their own situations.** Thus it is not just the amount of time spent in a session that matters to a parent, but *how* that time is spent.

This feedback guided the further shaping of the sessions in this guide to include less firsthand discovery and more information delivery. We focused on these two distinct kinds of information sought by parents: 1) the "experts' rationale" for why things are different than when they were in school; and 2) specific things parents can do with their children to promote academic achievement. Of course, keeping the sessions to a relatively short length has required that we rely on a full range of presentation techniques to accomplish these goals.

In This Guide: Parent Education Tools

In this guide are several kinds of tools for use in helping to educate parents of elementary-grade children about current educational practices in science and mathematics education, and about the power of parent involvement. All materials are designed to **provide parents with concrete and practical things they can do** that research has shown to be effective in helping children succeed academically. The variety of tools includes:

- **Information for Promotional Materials**—a series of short messages, to be included in school bulletins, newspaper notices, or promotional flyers to engage and interest parents and other caregivers in attending one or more of the parent sessions.

- **Parent Education Sessions**—step-by-step instructions for presenting parent education sessions, each about one hour and 15 minutes long. The sessions could be presented in the evening, on a Saturday, at the school, at a church or community center. Although they are designed to stand-alone, so a single workshop can be presented by itself, presenting more than one session creates a powerful sequence, especially in the suggested order. The three session topics are:

> **How Parents Make a Difference**
> **How Students Learn Best**
> **Testing: Knowing What Your Child Knows**

- **Take-Home Handouts**—these are clear, jargon-free, informational handouts to be given to participants at the parent education sessions. These handouts provide detailed information on what parents can do that makes a difference for children. Handouts include:

    What Parents Can Do to Make a Difference
    20 Ways to Support Your Children and Their School
    Four Common Ways Parents Discourage their Children
    Turning Discouragement into Encouragement
    Building a Strong Math/Science Foundation at Home
    Characteristics of Parenting that Promote Academic Success
    How Students Learn Best
    Sample Questions to Encourage Learning
    The Art of the Question
    What Are "Multiple Intelligences?"
    Multiple Intelligences and Your Children
    Assessing Your Children's Learning Habits
    Ways to Help Your Child Achieve High Standards
        for his/her Work
    Don't Believe Everything You Read in the News
    Assessing Your Coaching Skills
    Test-Taking

- **Engaging Messages**—these are a series of short digests of the research findings presented in the parent education sessions to be used in the school bulletin or other venues. Using these can serve to reach parents who weren't able to attend a session. They can also serve to interest parents who did not previously attend to come to future workshops where they can engage more interactively with the information.

- **Research References**—a selection of references relating to each of the three parent education sessions is included in this guide. We have starred (*) those references considered most useful and accessible for those parents and teachers who wish to find out more.

Making the Most Effective Use of These Materials

Parent education can be very powerful in transforming parent behaviors and, as such, is a critical piece of the equation needed to create vibrant and effective school communities. However, parent education by itself will not enable full parent involvement in a school community. There are many possible barriers to parent involvement, including: limited views of parent involvement (by teachers, administrators, or parents); discomfort with a partnership approach to education (by teachers or parents); time issues (particularly when both parents work outside the home or when there is only one parent in the home); and cultural and language barriers. Keys to overcoming these barriers include:

- Parents, teachers, and administrators believing in the value of parent involvement;

- Parents, teachers, and administrators understanding and respecting each other's roles in a child's education;

- Schools and teachers providing parents with the information they need to become active partners in their child's schooling and at home (such as how to help students with homework, information about the curriculum, things they can do at home together);

- Schools and teachers providing specific opportunities for parents to become involved at school (such as volunteer opportunities);

- Creating a variety of venues and locales for involvement so that all parents can find ways that are comfortable for them;

- Providing translations and translators as needed and possible.

It is intended that the tools and resources in this guide be used in flexible ways to help parents learn more about current educational practices in science and mathematics and how they as parents can help their children be successful. Ideally, these materials would be used as one piece of a larger program at a school that addresses the needs described above, with each of those audiences. If your school community has not yet built the attitudes, structures, and school practices that are inclusive of all parents, then perhaps these sessions can be used as a first step in that process. Each session description includes a section entitled, "Extending the Impact of this Session," designed to show how it could be used as part of a larger program.

Coordinating with School Staff. A good way to ensure that your presentation of these materials at a school fits in with and/or stimulates larger initiatives involving parent involvement is to schedule a time at a faculty meeting to share some of the details of what you will be presenting with the principal and teachers. The principal and the teachers can better support what you are doing when they know more about it. Teachers at one school, based on what they heard about these sessions at a faculty meeting, chose to make phone calls inviting parents of students in their class to attend. This was a highly effective recruitment method.

Timing of Sessions. Each of the three sessions is designed to be approximately one hour and 15 minutes long. Since an important part of each session involves discussion, it's difficult to determine an ideal time frame. While a session could easily be extended, it is our hope that a well-managed one hour and 15 minutes will be adequate to meet the goals of the session. **Be advised that the sessions are very full, and as the presenter you will need to actively "manage" the group in order to stay on schedule.** At the same time, the participatory nature of some of the session components will mean that you will need to strike a balance between keeping things on track and encouraging participation and free discussion. Parents will appreciate that their time is used well. We tried hard to balance an optimum amount of time for the learning experience with the very real pressures on parents' time.

When you advertise the specifics of the workshop, you might want to plan for an hour-and-a-half, and then start approximately 5–10 minutes late. This will minimize the number of people walking in late and ensure that you end on time. We have provided an "on-table handout" for each session—a short, engaging paragraph or two to start participants thinking. Those who come early or on time can read the handout and informally discuss it with other parents as they assemble.

Reaching All Parents. Reaching out to the broadest cross-section of parents should be your goal, in order to ensure the most effective education program with the greatest benefits for your school community. The barriers to parent involvement mentioned earlier are very real and need to be kept in mind as you plan your programs.

The materials in this guide have been designed, both in format and content, to appeal to a wide range of parents and other caregivers. We have attempted to keep the content of workshops and handouts relevant and interesting, while keeping the language in written materials accessible. The engaging messages are provided with the knowledge that not all parents can choose to make the time commitments required for meeting and reading.

"Our principal had us present these three sessions to the school staff first to great effect. Teachers themselves had the opportunity to learn some of what research says about parent involvement. They were better able to both create more ways to include parents and to time the communication of these opportunities."
—Two teachers in Washington

"We sent informational notes to the teachers before each session so they would know what the sessions were about and be prepared to field questions from the parents of their students."
—A parent leader in California

Be advised that the larger the size of your group, the harder it is to move through the agenda—especially if people have a lot to say. While we do advise managing the time well, it is rarely a good idea to cut off discussion prematurely. Be prepared to change your plan and decide to "cover" less material if your group is highly engaged and resists moving on to the next topic. Many presenters successfully split one session into two. One presenter combined two sessions into a successful half-day Saturday program.

Spanish versions of the handouts and other reading materials will be made available by GEMS shortly after this guide is published. All in-workshop activities are done in pairs or small groups, so English non-readers do not themselves have to read. The "engaging messages" and the "summing-up messages" were designed with the goal of promoting attendance at the parent education sessions, but with the awareness that these messages would be all that some parents will have time to see.

Customizing Presentations for the Parents in Your Community

In our initial field tests, conducted in a wide diversity of situations, we received little or no feedback related to these materials being too advanced. However, we did hear a consistent message that some parent audiences, usually those with more experience in talking and thinking about these issues, expected more information.

To address this, we have provided 10-minute optional sections at the end of two of the sessions (1 and 3), which present additional and more in-depth information. This will enable a presenter to start at the same place with all groups, but to go farther and faster when a group is comfortable in doing so. The feedback was clear that groups with some prior background *need* this additional information to consider their time well spent in having taken the time to attend. With a heterogeneous group, a presenter may want to play it by ear, and be prepared to go on if appropriate.

We think all parents will be interested in this information, but, especially with these additional sections, there is a lot of information "jammed" into each session. If it is all new to someone, it may be too much. In this case, some of the information can be presented at a later time.

If a majority of parents in your community are already confidently involved with their children's education, there may not be a need for presenting Session 1. Either go straight to Sessions 2 and 3 (both received excellent reviews from the full range of audiences) or consider expanding the optional section described at the end of Session 1 and/or doing some of the Going Further extensions mentioned there. **We have added Going Further ideas to all sessions with the idea that different presenters and different presentation situations will want and need a variety of approaches and materials.** Use these ideas to customize and further develop the three sessions as well as to create additional sessions.

Handout Heaven. Throughout the development of these materials, we heard loud and clear from parents and teachers that they considered the handouts to be extremely valuable. **Often a handout provides the practical actions that a parent can take, based on the research information that was presented during the session.** It was not uncommon for parents to hover around waiting to snatch them up at the end of each session! For this reason we have provided many take-home handouts. Depending on your situation you may or may not want to use all of them.

The handouts are written at a variety of levels (of depth and sophistication). While we have suggested that certain handouts be used with certain sessions, you will see that many are relevant to more than one session. Especially if you are only presenting one or two sessions, you may want to pick and choose from the entire collection of handouts. Use whatever seems right for your situation.

Setting a Comfortable Tone in the Sessions. There are many things that go into setting a comfortable tone, from how relaxed the presenter feels to providing refreshments. We have designed the sessions so: goals are shared at the beginning of each session (so participants don't have to wonder what will be happening and why); time is provided for participants to discuss; and much of the discussion is oriented to pairs and small groups (to reduce the pressure of talking in front of a large group). In addition, we suggest that you attempt to set as informal a tone as possible while still actively facilitating the session. Your active facilitation will help ensure that no one person dominates and that the discussion stays positive and on track.

Some presenters like to set up "ground rules" asking that participants: 1) ensure that everyone in their group has a chance to speak; and 2) when discussing problem situations, use the diplomatic approach of saying, "I know someone who..." or "I have had the experience that..." This heads off the uncomfortable situation of having a parent single out teachers by name. Other presenters have arranged ahead of time to have teachers and/or parents they know sit at individual tables and serve in the role of facilitator. Still others ask for a volunteer from each table to play that role.

It works well to let groups know that this is a time for everyone (including you) to learn from each other.

Recruitment Strategies. The ways that you use these materials can further affect how successful they are. There is a lot known about recruitment strategies. For instance, the location at which you hold the parent education sessions matters. In some communities, the school site is a good site. In other com-

We heard from many people that they used the handouts to support more than just these sessions. One presenter provided them to parents who came to Family Math and Science nights. Another presenter passed them out at PTA meetings.

One presenter set up a resource table at each session. She had things the participants could choose to take (like these handouts) as well as other resources on parenting, school, homework, etc. that participants could peruse.

"These presentations are so positive. I was worried ahead of time. So often in our community it's 'us against them' (teachers against parents). I really felt like I bonded with the parents and that they left wanting to partner with their children's teachers. These sessions helped communicate that together we will make the difference. "
—A teacher leader in California

munities, holding sessions at other community sites—such as at the location of afterschool care programs or at a church—is more productive. Most parents we polled in our communities felt fine about coming to school, but were not interested in having the session be part of the PTA structure, as this structure can sometimes have the feel of an exclusive group. If you don't already know the best ways to attract people to events in your school community, you might want to find out the most appealing location by conducting a written or phone survey.

Using phone trees so the word can be spread from parent to parent can be a very effective recruitment strategy. Parents can offer to give each other rides as appropriate. Relying on existing social structure is a powerful way to stimulate attendance, such as asking each parent who came to the first workshop to recruit one other parent to attend the second workshop with them. Personal invitations by teachers can also be effective. Providing transportation, food, and daycare are all things that may be important to ensuring broad attendance. We know of a school that uses door prizes and raffles at parent meetings. Another advertised the opportunity for kids to see a newly-released children's video while their parents attended the session. Other sites have had teachers or parents offer science and math activities for children in one room while their parents participate in these parent education sessions in another. The sites who did this had record turnouts!

Several schools mentioned how they had great success when they sent home reminder notes the day before a session and/or made reminder calls to certain parents early on the day of the session.

There is no one winning formula for reaching a broad cross-section of parents—every school community is different. Capitalize on what is already known about successful strategies for your particular community, and build on that knowledge to come up with new ways that work.

The Rewards!

Not only has research clearly established the rewards to individual students of having their parents more involved with their education and schooling, **there is strong evidence that parent involvement is one of the key factors that determines if a school is an "effective" school. Studies show that parent involvement greatly improves the overall quality of schools.**

Schools that find ways to work well with families have higher student achievement, improved teacher morale, higher ratings of teachers by parents, more support from families, and better reputations in the community. This has been shown to be the case in both low and high resource communities.

While parent education is only a piece of the bigger parent involvement picture, it is a critical piece. It is our hope that these flexible tools will contribute to the greater goal of preparing parents, teachers, and administrators to work together as partners in ensuring that *all* children have the greatest advantages in achieving success.

Note: The following are provided as examples to inspire your own promotional announcements. Modify and expand them, depending on which sessions you are presenting, and on your own unique school situation and audiences.

MAKING A DIFFERENCE IN YOUR CHILD'S EDUCATION

A Series of Free Presentations

for Parents at _____

Interested in what research shows about the power of parents and other adult caregivers to make a difference in a child's education? Wondering about some of the new ways science and math are taught and what research says about how students learn best? How is your child doing in math and science? How do you know? How could you find out more? How can you help your child have the greatest academic success?

Achievement in science and math can have a big impact on career choices and your child's future. To learn more, you are invited to attend a special series of free presentations on these three topics.

Tuesday, Oct. 20: How Parents Make a Difference

Tuesday, Oct. 27: How Students Learn Best

Tuesday, Nov. 3: Testing: Knowing What Your Child Knows

In the _____ from **7:30 p.m.–9:00 p.m.**

Sessions will be presented by _____.

Feel free to come to one or more sessions.

Childcare provided.

How Parents Make a Difference

Interested in what research shows about the power of parents and other adult caregivers to make a difference in your child's education? Come to the first of three sessions for parents at _____, next Tuesday,

October 20th, from 7:30 p.m.–9:00 p.m.

Childcare provided.

How Students Learn Best

Learn and discuss some of the rationale behind various teaching strategies and their strengths in helping students learn. What does research say about different learning styles? Come to the second session for parents at _____, on Tuesday,

October 27th, from 7:30 p.m.–9:00 p.m.

Childcare provided.

Testing: Knowing What Your Child Knows

In recent years, a lot has changed in the often controversial areas of testing and assessment of students' academic achievement. Come learn the rationale behind some of these changes and gain deeper insight into your child's own school work. Discuss how to interpret news reports on test scores. This is the third of three sessions for parents at _____, on Tuesday,

November 3rd, from 7:30 p.m.–9:00 p.m.

Childcare provided.

Parent Partners

When parents are partners
Lo and behold—
Schools and their teachers
New wings will unfold
Community spirit
Will rise to new heights
When parents are partners
Things tend to go right.

When parents are partners
Research does show
Test scores improve
Student learning does grow
Everyone benefits
From breath of fresh air
When parents are partners
Kids know we care.

When parents are partners
Kids learn to read
Teachers teach better
Planting the seed
Lifelong love of learning
Sprouts in classrooms
When parents are partners
Our children's minds bloom.

When parents are partners
We say in shorthand
But it's not only parents
Whose role can expand
All other caregivers,
Who help meet a need—
When we work as partners
Our schools will succeed!

Session 1:
How Parents Make a Difference

Overview

This session is highly effective with parents who don't know how to guide, facilitate, and support their child's education and/or who need encouragement about the positive things that they are already doing. Ninety-five percent of our field test audience were enthusiastic about the value of this session. If a majority of parents in your community are already confidently involved with their children's education, there may not be a need for presenting this session. Either go straight to one of the other two sessions in this guide or consider doing some of the Going Further extensions mentioned on pages 27–28 and/or expanding the optional section described at the end of this session.

In this workshop, the presenter provides participants with the overwhelming evidence that any parent/adult caregiver can provide the single biggest advantage to their child's academic success regardless of situation, background, or education.

Beginning with an acknowledgment of the very real barriers to parent involvement, the session goes on to focus on an exploration of concrete and specific ideas for actions, many of them small, and many occurring outside of school. Participants learn the positive effect these actions have been shown to have on children's academic success.

Participants discuss new actions they would be comfortable in undertaking and generate a list of the kinds of support that they would need from schools, teachers, and others to expand their "comfort zone" to include even more ways of becoming involved with their children's education and schooling. As a result of this activity, participants typically feel surprised at how many important things they are currently doing and energized about the possibilities for doing more.

The concept is introduced that a child's "education" and "schooling" are two different things. While schooling is a critically important piece of a child's education, it is just a piece. Teachers are in charge of our children's schooling; parents facilitate, support, and advocate for their children's total education in many ways. This workshop helps participants know the various arenas and many ways in which they can provide their children with the needed support.

The workshop ends with the optional presentation of what researchers have found to be the characteristics of parenting that promote academically successful students. This ten-minute optional ending to the session provides additional information for groups who have digested the main portion of the session. Many groups are hungry for this additional information and ready for it at this time. Other groups may benefit from hearing it at another time. If you have an "experienced" audience, who move more quickly through earlier portions, you might want to plan to present this additional ten-minute portion within the 75 minutes of this session. Or you can play it by ear, and continue on if you have time and the group has interest. Our experience indicated that some audiences want this additional information.

Extending the impact of this session

This session will be valuable to participants in helping each of them know what things they can do most easily to increase their involvement. The input from participants can also be used to inform school practices, extending this value to the entire school community. Research shows that parent involvement is maximized not only by changing parent behaviors but by changing teacher behaviors and school practices as well.

Thus, the ideas collected from parents about what the school and/or teachers could do to help support their increased involvement can supply key information for each school site. For instance, teachers could decide to provide some guidance to parents who are wondering how to be most effective in helping their children with homework. Or, in response to parents not knowing how they could be involved in the classroom beyond providing snack, a school could set up more structured opportunities, both during and after the school day, for parents to become involved with academic activities.

If possible, use this session as a key step in the important process by which teachers, principals, and schools learn how they can help parents and other adult caregivers know how to be involved with their children's schooling and feel welcome in doing so.

Time Frame

Total Workshop: 75 minutes
    Introduction (10 minutes)
    Schooling vs. Education (10 minutes)
    Research/Action Strips Activity (20 minutes)
    Comfort Zone Discussion (20 minutes)
    Optional: Characteristics of Parenting that Promote Academic
        Success (10 minutes—note: groups that skip this portion
        are happy to have the extra discussion time in earlier
        portions of the session)
    Conclusion (5 minutes)

What You Need

To prepare the materials:
❑ 1 large-tipped marker
❑ 1 paper cutter or a pair of scissors

For the presenter:
❑ 1 each of the following overhead transparencies
   (masters on pages 39–45):
   • 1. Barriers to Parent Involvement
   • 2. Less Significant Factors
   • 3. Most Significant Factors
   • 4. Schooling vs. Education
   • 5. Home/School Venn Diagram
   • 6. Characteristics of Parenting that Promote
     Academic Success
   • 7. Three Common Parenting Styles
❑ overhead projector
❑ blank overhead transparencies and an overhead pen or
   1 large-tipped marker, butcher paper, and masking tape
❑ extension cord (optional)

For each participant:
❑ 1 of the following on-table handout:
   • How Parents Make a Difference (master on page 46)
❑ 1 of each of the following take-home handouts:
   • 1. What Parents Can Do to Make a Difference
     (master on pages 47–48)
   • 2. 20 Ways to Support Your Children and Their School
     (master on pages 49–51)
   • 3. Four Common Ways Parents Discourage their Children
     (master on pages 52–53)
   • 4. Turning Discouragement into Encouragement
     (master on pages 54–58)
   • 5. Building a Strong Math/Science Foundation at Home
     (master on pages 59–62)
   • 6. Characteristics of Parenting that Promote Academic
     Success (master on page 63)
   • 7. Recommended Family Education Programs (master on
     page 64)
   • 8. Session 1: Research References (master on pages 65–66)

For each group of 4–6 participants:
❏ 1 legal-size envelope
❏ 1 set of action/research strips (see Getting Ready #3; two-sided masters on pages 29–38)
❏ 1 large piece of paper (approximately 2' x 3') to make Venn diagram (Note: a sheet of chart paper, a piece of butcher paper, or about six 8½" x 11" sheets of paper taped together will work. The exact size does not matter.)

Getting Ready

Before the Day of the Workshop

1. Duplicate handouts. Decide which take-home handouts you would like to make available to participants. For each participant, duplicate one copy of the on-table handout and whichever of the eight take-home handouts you have decided to use.

2. Make overhead transparencies. Make one of each of the seven overhead transparencies.

3. Make strips. Make one set of action/research strips for each group of 4–6 participants. To make one set: duplicate the two-sided masters on pages 29–38. Using a paper cutter, cut the pages into strips so one two-sided statement is on each strip. Put one complete set of strips in an envelope. You may choose to use colored paper in making the strips.

4. Make Venn diagrams. Make one Venn diagram for each group of 4–6 participants. To make one diagram: on a piece of paper approximately 2' x 3' use a marker to draw two overlapping circles. Label the left circle as "HOME" and the right circle as "SCHOOL."

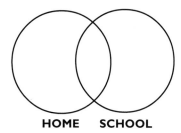

HOME   SCHOOL

Immediately Before the Workshop

1. Set up the room. Arrange the room so that groups of 4–6 participants can sit at a table together. If you are in a classroom, move desks together to make "tables." Tables should be oriented so that all of the table groups can join a large group discussion.

2. Set up the overhead projector. Set up the overhead projector so that you can project onto a screen, white board, light-colored wall, or large sheet of butcher paper. Put the seven overhead transparencies in order next to the overhead projector. If you are planning to record the support list from the comfort zone discussion on blank transparencies, have the blank transparencies and overhead pen nearby as well.

3. Set out on-table handout. Place one copy of the handout, How Parents Make a Difference at each seat, so that parents will have something to look at when they first arrive.

4. Assemble remaining workshop materials. Have easily accessible (but not yet at their seats) all of the remaining workshop materials:

- envelopes containing action/research strips
- Venn diagrams
- take-home handouts

Introduction (10 minutes)

1. Introduce yourself. Introduce yourself and the context of the workshop. Tell participants that this session is intended to: a) present what research says about the topic of how parents make a difference in their children's academic success; and b) provide a forum for discussion about important educational topics. While this session was designed from the perspective of mathematics and science, and elementary-aged students, most of what will be presented can be generalized to all of learning.

Point out that an hour and fifteen minutes is not long to accomplish the goals of the workshop, and that you have a tight schedule planned. In order to be able to end on time, you will appreciate their cooperation and attention in the workshop.

Some parents may be interested in pursuing educational research findings on the crucial importance of parent involvement in more detail. A Research Reference list is provided for this and the other two presentations included in this guide. You may want to mention this to parents up front.

2. Acknowledge barriers to involvement. Explain that as busy parents, we all know some of the practical barriers to getting involved with our children's schooling and education. Show overhead transparency #1.

Barriers to Parent Involvement

· Time issues (particularly when both parents work outside the home or when there is only one parent in the home);

· Cultural and language barriers (many of us aren't comfortable at our children's school, especially if we weren't comfortable at school as children, or if language or cultural differences are an obstacle).

While it is important to acknowledge the very real barriers to parent involvement, it is our recommendation that you head off a deeper discussion of these. What is designed to be an empowering session focused on solutions could easily degenerate into a complaining session. This is not to minimize the realities of the barriers to involvement, rather to use the limited time parents have available to attend sessions like these, in the more productive activity of finding comfortable ways that each individual can confront their own barriers.

These obstacles are very real.

3. Share key research finding—you can make a difference.
Say, that while we may be experts on the barriers(!), what many
of us don't know is the **overwhelming conclusion to several
decades of research on parent involvement and student
achievement—that parent involvement is the most accurate
predictor of students' academic success.** Refer to on-table
handout.

There is a great deal of research focusing on the characteristics
of: students who succeed in school vs. students who don't;
parents of successful students vs. parents of unsuccessful
students; and effective schools vs. ineffective schools. The
research focuses on what difference and commonalities there
are in order to determine the specific attributes of effective
schools and of families whose children get ahead. The ways in
which parents/adult caregivers were involved with their
children was shown to be the single most important factor.

4. Less significant factors. Acknowledge that there are
certainly other important factors which affect a child's
achievement related to the details of parents' background or
current situation (all of which are hard or impossible to
change). These have been shown to be less significant. Show
overhead transparency #2.

Less Significant Factors

- parent's level of education
- 1 or 2 parents active in raising a child
- family's socio-economic status
- English-speaking household
- size of family
- child's own interests, talents, and abilities

---

5. Most significant factors. The most important factor are
parents' expectations, attitudes, and actions. Show overhead
transparency #3.

Most Significant Factors

1) home environment that encourages learning
2) high expectations by parents and caregivers
3) involvement of parents/caregivers in children's
   education at school and in the community

Let the participants know that they can make the *single biggest
difference* in their child's academic success, regardless of their
own situation, background, or education.

6. Outline goal for the day. Tell participants that today they will focus on the specific things that research has shown that have enabled parents of all backgrounds to overcome some of these barriers; some of which are in ways that don't take much time or effort, many of which take place outside of school.

Schooling vs. Education (10 minutes)

1. Icebreaker. Ask participants to spend just a few minutes talking with the person next to them. Have them share one thing they currently do to support their child's education.

2. Share ways they support. After several minutes, regain the group's attention. Ask for several volunteers to share what they said with the whole group. If the examples that are shared represent both ways of supporting a child in school and ways of supporting a child's overall education, make that observation as a transition to the next step. ["I notice some of these great examples are ways of supporting a child's schooling and some are related more broadly to a child's education."] If the examples are in either the "schooling" arena or the larger "education arena," go ahead and make that observation. ["I notice that all of these great examples are ways of supporting a child's schooling."]

3. Define arenas of schooling and education. Point out a difference between "schooling" and "education." Show overhead transparency #4.

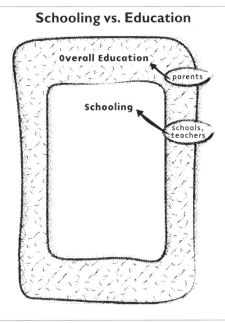

Schooling vs. Education

Overall Education

parents

Schooling

schools, teachers

Share that many of us think of "school" and our child's "schooling" as his or her education. While schooling is a critically important part of a person's education, it is just one part. A child's education encompasses all of the learning that she or he does in life. Teachers and schools are in charge of our children's schooling. Parents facilitate and support their children's total education in many ways.

There are many inputs that all contribute to a child's total education: community services, extracurricular activities, communicating openly with your child about values, role models, television, peers, and more. All we've learned through research shows that a parent's active management of a child's whole education is key.

Explain that in this session you will focus on things parents and caregivers already do and/or can do to support and facilitate their children's schooling and the things they can do to support and facilitate their children's total education.

Research/Action Strips Activity (20 minutes)

1. What's on the strips. Explain that each group of 4–6 parents will get a set of several dozen two-sided "research/action strips." (Hold up an envelope containing the strips.) On one side of a strip is a specific concrete action that a parent can take; on the other side is the research evidence that shows its specific effectiveness.

2. What you do with the strips. Tell them that when they get these strips, they should work in pairs to read both sides of the strip. Then together decide where on this diagram to put the strip. Show overhead transparency #5.

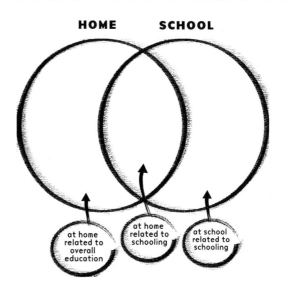

3. Explain Venn diagram. Say that some of them might remember this kind of diagram from when they were in school. Explain that it's called a **Venn diagram.** It has two overlapping circles. One is labeled "Home" and one is labeled "School."

Ask them to place a strip that describes something you would do at your child's school related to his/her schooling in the circle labeled "school." Place a strip that describes something you would do at home, related to home activities and a child's overall education in the circle labeled "home." In the overlapping area of the two circles place things that you would do at home that support your child's schooling. Explain that some of these strips could be placed in more than one part of the diagram, so they should not worry too much about where they place it. Their goal is to read and discuss both sides of the strips, and think about whether it is related to schooling or overall education, whether it happens at home or at school.

You will need to emphasize more than once that the exact placement of these strips is unimportant.

Ideally there would be a three-circle Venn diagram with the overlapping circles representing Home, School, and Community. However this creates a fairly complicated sorting exercise (going from a total of three possible categories to seven), and distinguishing the different categories is not the main purpose of the activity. Some people are happy with the two categories: Home and School. Others prefer to rename the categories Outside School and School, or Home/Community and School. Feel free to adapt as you see fit.

4. Summarize by saying:

- Place in HOME circle if activity is:
  at home, related to home and overall education

- Place in SCHOOL circle if activity is:
  at school, related to schooling

- Place in overlap between HOME and SCHOOL if activity is:
  at home but related to schooling

5. Check for questions. Ask if there are questions about what they are to do.

6. Have them begin the activity. Distribute diagrams and strips and have them begin. Let them know they will have about 15 minutes to conduct the activity. Not all groups need the same amount of time to do this activity. Pay attention to the level of engagement. If the group seems "through," even though they are not finished, go ahead and end the activity and use the extra time for some of the reflection that follows.

You might want to let participants know that you will be giving them a take-home handout listing the information that appears on the strips.

7. Circulate among the groups as they work, commenting and clarifying instructions as needed. Listen to what's being discussed.

Comfort Zone Discussion (20 minutes)

1. Comfort zone. When most of the groups have read and categorized most of the strips, or about 30 minutes from the end of the workshop, get the group's attention. Introduce the notion of a comfort zone—that research shows it's important that parents begin by participating in their child's education in ways they find that are comfortable.

2. Choose comfortable new actions. Ask participants to choose several strips describing actions they aren't currently doing, but seem comfortable for them to begin to do. Ask that they discuss them in pairs.

Depending on your group, you may choose to actually have people write down an action they would like to begin doing as a private goal that they take away with them at the end of the workshop. For some groups this might seem less appropriate.

3. Check for questions. Ask if there are questions about what they are to do.

4. Have pairs begin the discussion. Let them know they will have about 5–10 minutes to conduct the activity.

5. Support needed. Get the group's attention. Ask them to discuss in their small groups things that teachers, schools, or others might be able to do that would expand their comfort zone—increasing the number of actions they would feel comfortable in doing. As parents or other caregivers, what help and support might they want? Let them know they will have about 10 minutes to discuss and that you will ask each group to share some of their ideas.

6. Make support list. After about 10 minutes, get the group's attention one last time. Ask people to raise their hands and report on things they discussed that teachers, schools, or others could do to support their involvement as parents/caregivers. Record these ideas on a blank overhead transparency or sheet of butcher paper.

Conclude by saying that increasing parent involvement and changing parent behaviors is certainly one side of the equation. Changing school practices to be more inclusive and supportive of parent involvement is the other side of the equation

7. Show take-home handout. Hold up the take-home handout entitled, What Parents Can Do to Make a Difference. Tell them that this has the information that was on the strips: concrete actions they can take to increase their child's academic success. Tell them that you will distribute this handout at the end.

In certain situations, this can be a sensitive discussion and turn into a heated complaining session if it is not carefully facilitated. A common theme for parents is wanting more communication with teachers and the school. Do your best to steer this discussion in a positive way, helping parents generate ideas for solutions. Some workshop leaders have chosen to set ground rules, such as not mentioning specific teachers' names, in order to keep the conversation at the level of actions and supports.

These ideas for the kinds of support that parents perceive that they need in order to be more involved with their child's schooling and education provide key information for schools. If appropriate, tell participants that this information will be shared with the principal and the other teachers at the school in order to help build the kinds of support that parents feel they need.

Optional: Characteristics of Parenting that Promote Academic Success (10 minutes)

1. Parenting styles. In addition to the research about specific actions parents can take, there is research showing that certain parenting styles are more effective in producing children who are successful in school. Researchers have identified three fundamental dimensions of parenting that affect academic performance and differentiate parents of successful students from parents of less successful students. Show overhead transparency #6.

Characteristics of Parenting that Promote Academic Success

Acceptance <————————>Rejectance

Firmness <————————>Leniency

Autonomy<————————>Control

---

2. Explain how each dimension is defined.

- Acceptance is defined as parents who are involved, responsive, liberal with praise, and affectionate. The other end of the spectrum is defined as the opposite.

- Firmness is defined as parents who set clear limits, have high standards, have consequences for behavior, and are consistent.

- Autonomy is defined as parents who value self expression, and don't expect a child to hold the same opinions in order to have their love. Parents who value autonomy emphasize independence over obedience.

3. Share the target for parents. Point out that all of us fall somewhere between the two extremes of each range (and this certainly varies from day to day!). **Research has shown that parents who are closer to the left hand side of each dimension, over time, have children who are more successful in school.**

4. The sum is greater than the parts. Further, the research has shown that the combination of these positive dimensions of parenting have a greater effect when they occur together. For instance, a child whose parents were accepting *and* firm *and* supportive of autonomy benefited more than a child whose parents were accepting but not firm, or firm but not supportive of autonomy.

Please Note: This optional portion of the presentation is intended to provide interested audiences with even more food for thought about parenting. It is based on voluminous research, and we have found raising it a good way to involve parents in becoming more conscious about the relation of parenting to their child's success in school. It is possible that in some settings individual parents may react defensively. If you think that may be the case in your situation, you could choose not to present it, schedule a separate session, or adapt in some other way. It may be important to emphasize that these categories are based on published research and that they are used here as a way to get people thinking, not as a judgment of anyone's personal or cultural practices, and not as a statement of "right" or "wrong." In the Research References section, see particularly the listing under Steinberg for more information.

5. Parenting styles. The research goes on to identify three common patterns of parenting that have become known as parenting styles. Most parents fall in one of the following three patterns. Show overhead transparency #7.

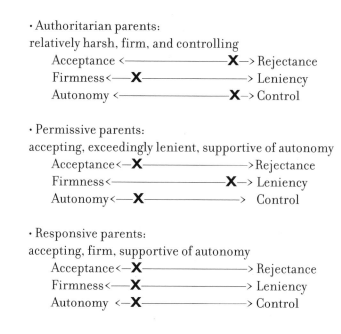

Three Common Parenting Styles

· Authoritarian parents:
relatively harsh, firm, and controlling
Acceptance <———————**X**—> Rejectance
Firmness<——**X**——————> Leniency
Autonomy <———————**X**—> Control

· Permissive parents:
accepting, exceedingly lenient, supportive of autonomy
Acceptance<—**X**——————>Rejectance
Firmness<——————**X**—> Leniency
Autonomy<—**X**——————> Control

· Responsive parents:
accepting, firm, supportive of autonomy
Acceptance<—**X**——————> Rejectance
Firmness<——**X**——————> Leniency
Autonomy <—**X**——————> Control

These three different parenting styles reflect very different values and beliefs about what is best for the child. For instance, while authoritarian parents often appear aloof or cold to a child, it is not because they don't love the child, but rather that they believe that too much affection and praise will interfere with a child's positive development. Similar examples can be given for motivation of parents who choose to be lenient or controlling.

Research has consistently shown that children of "responsive" parents are more self-reliant, more cheerful, more socially skilled, more curious, more persistent, more responsible, and more self-controlled when compared to their peers whose parents are "permissive" or "authoritarian."

Some presenters prefer to use the term "respectful" instead of "responsive." This word may be more accessible for some audiences, although it should not imply that those with other parenting styles don't "respect" their children. "Responsive" has a nice feeling of interaction associated with it. In any case, and as with the unusual word "rejectance," we've chosen to follow the terminology used in the main source for this analysis (*Beyond the Classroom: Why School Reform has Failed and What Parents Need To Do,* by Laurence Steinberg, Simon & Schuster, New York, 1996).

6. Show other take-home handout. Hold up the take-home handout entitled Characteristics of Parenting that Promote Academic Success. Tell them that this has information about the characteristics of parenting that increase a child's academic success and that you will distribute this handout at the end.

Conclusion (5 minutes)

1. Reiterate the key point. Explain that one of the goals of this activity is to help parents know how much they are already doing. The point is NOT to imply that any of us can do it all, but that there are many little things that can be done that together can make a big difference. **As parents and caregivers, they can make the single biggest difference in their child's academic success, regardless of their own situation, background, or education.**

2. Distribute take-home sheets. Set the take-home handouts and the Research Reference list on a table so parents can take what they'd like when they leave.

3. If you're planning to present other sessions, let them know when and where, and encourage them to bring other parents.

4. Be sure to thank all the participants for coming and for the ideas and comments they've shared. If you have a feedback or evaluation form for the participants, urge them to complete it so presentations can be improved in the future.

Going Further

1. In the context of an ongoing series of sessions with the same group of parents, participants could create their own action plans for how they would like to increase their participation in their children's education and schooling.

2. Provide participants with a chance to digest and interact with the information you presented about the characteristics of parenting that promote academic success. Have them discuss each characteristic (acceptance/rejectance; firmness/leniency; autonomy/control). Focus the discussion by providing scenarios of a child's behavior and asking participants to come up with a parent's response to that scenario that is accepting as contrasted to rejecting; or firm as contrasted to lenient; or autonomous as contrasted to controlling. Possible scenarios could include:

   a. Your child comes home with a disappointing report card. Some parts of it are fine but others indicate that your child may not be trying as hard as he can. What would an "accepting" response be? What would a "rejecting" response be?

b. Your child dislikes doing her homework and often leaves it to the end of the evening when she and you are tired. Together, you set up a plan for regularly completing homework after school. In the first week of the plan, your child requests to do "special" things on two of the five days. What would a "firm" response be? What would a "lenient" response be?

c. Your child is signed up for a weekly basketball clinic prior to basketball season. He is very talented and the coach says that if he works hard he could make the varsity team. He likes playing basketball—it's his sport. He wanted to sign up for the clinic, but now that it's underway, he feels like he has no free time. He complains about going and looks for excuses of why he can't go or must leave early. You want him to try his hardest and be the best he can be. You also want him to have the option of playing on the varsity team. What would be a "controlling" way of handling this situation? What would be an "autonomous" way of handling it?

3. Several of the take-home handouts would provide great read-and-discuss situations for groups of four participants. For instance, the handouts Four Common Ways Parents Discourage their Children and Turning Discouragement into Encouragement provide more information on questions that often come up in the session, such as, "How do you determine what is a high but not-unrealistic expectation for your child?" These kinds of open-ended discussions can prove very fruitful, especially when participants can choose the topic they want to discuss.

Establish a daily family routine. Get children ready for school every morning. Be firm about times to get up and go to bed.

- -

Communicate through questioning and conversation. Use reference materials and the library to find answers to questions and to pursue interests.

- -

Have dinner as a family. Discuss the day over dinner.

- -

Tell stories and share problems. Reflect on the lessons learned through daily experiences.

- -

Read to your children and have them read to you. Talk together about what you have read. Write letters, lists, and messages.

- -

Recognize and encourage special talents. Enroll your child in sports programs or music lessons.

- -

Expose your child to many learning opportunities outside of school, such as visiting museums and nature centers, going to concerts, and talking about current events.

 Families whose children do well in school have a home life with a daily family routine that helps their children be prepared to learn at school.

- -

 Families whose children do well in school use community resources for family needs and have a home life that includes reading, writing, and discussions among family members.

- -

 Families whose children do well in school have a home life with a daily family routine and a chance to talk with adults.

- -

 Families whose children do well in school model the values of learning, self-discipline, and hard work at home.

- -

 Families whose children do well in school have a home life that includes reading, writing, and discussions among family members.

- -

 A child's education encompasses all of the learning she or he does in life. Parents facilitate and support their children's total education in many ways. Schooling is a critically important piece of a child's education—but it is not the only piece.

- -

 A child's education encompasses all of the learning she or he does in life. Parents facilitate and support their children's total education in many ways. Schooling is a critically important piece of a child's education—but it is not the only piece.

Use community services, such as Boys and Girls clubs, libraries, the "Y."

· ·

Listen to and talk with your child about things that are important to you both.

· ·

Have high expectations and show interest in your child's progress at school. Also have high expectations about your child's education after high school and career choices.

· ·

Set goals and standards that are appropriate for children's age and maturity.

· ·

Inform friends and family about your child's successes.

· ·

Discuss the value of a good education and possible career options.

· ·

Introduce children to role models and mentors.

 Families whose children do well in school use community resources for family needs.

 Families whose children do well in school have a home life that includes discussions among family members.

 Families whose children do well in school express high but realistic expectations for achievement. Children "get ahead" in life when their families stress high grades, pay attention to what's happening at school, suggest options for education after high school, and discuss possible future occupations.

 Families whose children do well in school express high but realistic expectations for achievement. They encourage children's growth and progress in school.

 Families whose children do well in school encourage children's growth and progress in school and communicate that they value education.

 Families who stress high grades, pay attention to what's happening at school, suggest options for education after high school, and discuss possible future occupations have children who "get ahead" in life.

 Families whose children do well in school model the values of learning, self-discipline, and hard work at home and in the community.

Share your knowledge with your child's class (your job, a skill you have, an interest).

. . . .

Work with small groups or individuals in the classroom. Help with tutorial and remedial work (your own child's or others').

. . . .

Assist teachers by obtaining and preparing class materials.

. . . .

Serve on collaborative decision-making committees.

. . . .

Help with field trips and extracurricular activities.

. . . .

Help arrange "open house" activities and meetings.

. . . .

Explain school programs and needs to the community (your next door neighbor, the School Board, community organizations, etc.).

Students develop better attitudes toward their school and school work when their parents are involved with the school's instructional program. This effect has been found to carry over to benefit all students, not just those whose parents volunteered in the classroom. Schools with active parent involvement have been shown to be more effective than those without.

Schools with the most successful programs provide a range of different ways for parents to participate. Parent involvement greatly improves the overall quality of schools. This has been shown to be the case in both low and high resource communities.

Schools with the most successful programs provide a range of different ways for parents to participate. Parent involvement greatly improves the overall quality of schools. This has been shown to be the case in both low and high resource communities.

Schools with the most successful programs provide a range of different ways for parents to participate. Parent involvement greatly improves the overall quality of schools. This has been shown to be the case in both low and high resource communities.

Schools with the most successful programs provide a range of different ways for parents to participate. Parent involvement greatly improves the overall quality of schools. This has been shown to be the case in both low and high resource communities.

Schools with the most successful programs provide a range of different ways for parents to participate. Parent involvement greatly improves the overall quality of schools. This has been shown to be the case in both low and high resource communities.

Students develop better attitudes toward their school and school work when their parents are involved with the school's instructional program. This effect has been found to carry over to benefit all students, not just those whose parents volunteered in the classroom. Schools with active parent involvement have been shown to be more effective than those without.

Help with homework.

. . . .

Stay in touch with teachers and school staff.

. . . .

Respect and understand a teacher's role in your child's education, as well as your own role.

. . . .

Talk directly with your child's teacher about concerns you might have.

. . . .

Talk directly with the teacher to share what your joint expectations for your child's growth and progress are.

. . . .

Give spelling or math drills.

. . . .

Visit the classroom. Volunteer at the school.

 Families whose children do well in school encourage their children's growth and progress in school.

 The most powerful combination for learning is the family and school working together. Parents and teachers need to view themselves as partners in children's education.

 Children's attitudes and performance in school increase when parents and teachers understand and respect each other, share similar expectations, and stay in communication.

 How parents and teachers relate affects children's attitudes and performance in school. Children who conclude "my parent and my teacher are working this out together" will be more successful than children who conclude "my parent doesn't like my teacher/school."

 Students' attitudes and performance in school improve when parents and teachers share the same expectations. The most powerful combination for learning is the family and school working together. Parents and teachers need to view themselves as partners in children's education.

 Families whose children do well in school encourage their children's growth and progress in school.

 Students develop better attitudes toward their school and school work when their parents are involved with the school's instructional program. This effect has been found to carry over to benefit all students, not just those whose parents volunteered in the classroom. Schools with active parent involvement have been shown to be more effective than those without.

Provide time and a quiet place to study.

· ·

Assign responsibility for household chores.

· ·

Set limits on TV watching.

· ·

Arrange for after-school activities and supervised care.
Check up on children when parents are not home.

· ·

Maintain a warm and supportive home.

· ·

Families whose children do well in school encourage their children's growth and progress in school. This includes helping them develop good study habits and creating an environment where they can do their school work.

Families whose children do well in school help their children be prepared to learn at school.

Families whose children do well in school monitor out-of-school activities. Too much time spent watching TV can reduce time available for more active learning situations, such as social, physical, and educational play.

Families whose children do well in school monitor out-of-school activities.

Families whose children do well in school have a home life with a daily family routine and a family that supports the child's growth and development.

Barriers to Parent Involvement

• Time issues

   (particularly when both parents work outside the home or when there is only one parent in the home);

• Cultural and language barriers

   (many of us aren't comfortable at our children's school, especially if we weren't comfortable at school as children, or if language or cultural differences are an obstacle).

Less Significant Factors

- parent's level of education

- 1 or 2 parents active in raising a child

- family's socio-economic status

- English-speaking household

- size of family

- child's own interests, talents, and abilities

Most Significant Factors

1) home environment that encourages learning

2) high expectations by parents and caregivers

3) involvement of parents/caregivers in
   children's education at school and in
   the community

Schooling vs. Education

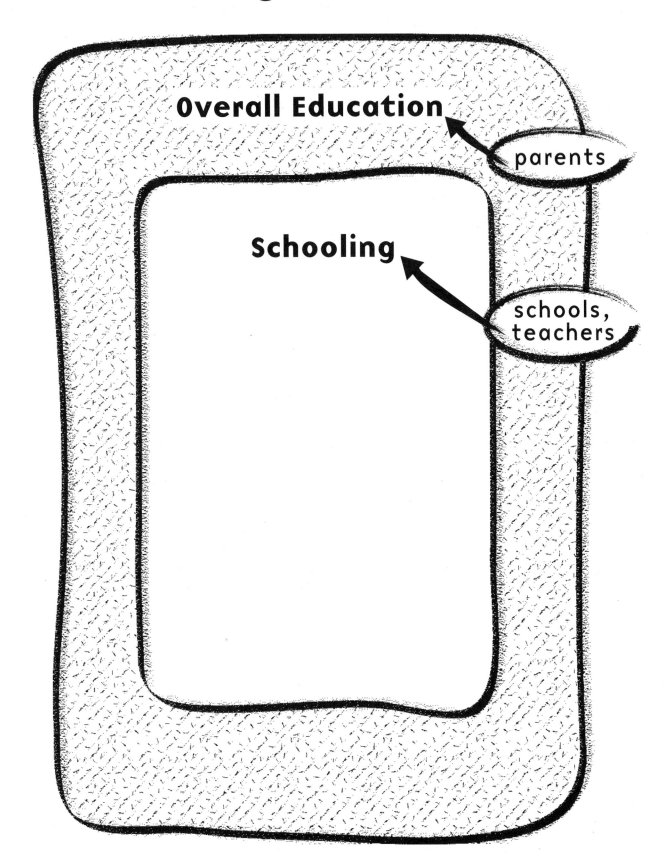

Overall Education

Schooling

parents

schools, teachers

HOME   SCHOOL

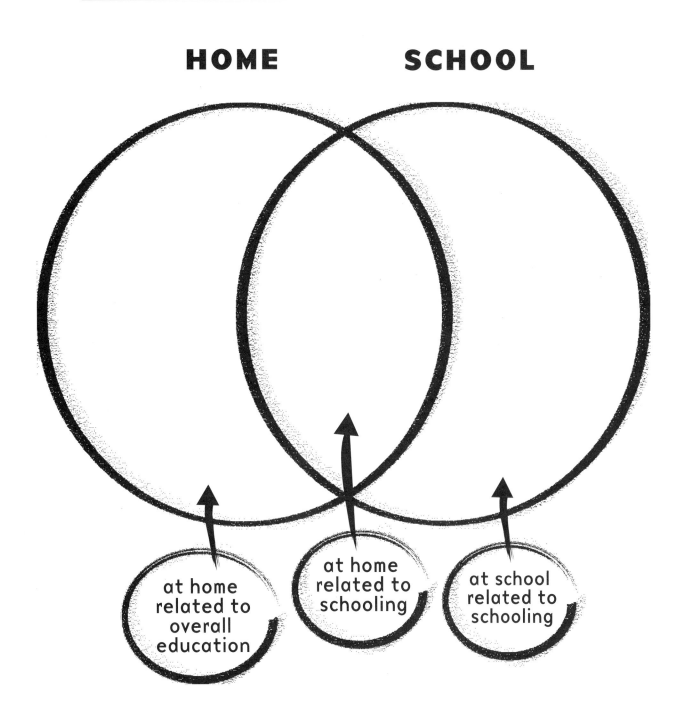

at home related to overall education

at home related to schooling

at school related to schooling

Characteristics of Parenting that Promote Academic Success

Acceptance <————————> Rejectance

Firmness <————————> Leniency

Autonomy <————————> Control

Three Common Parenting Styles

- ## Authoritarian parents:
relatively harsh, firm, and controlling

Acceptance <————————**X**—> Rejectance

Firmness <—**X**————————————> Leniency

Autonomy<————————**X**—> Control

- ## Permissive parents:
accepting, exceedingly lenient, supportive of autonomy

Acceptance <—**X**————————————> Rejectance

Firmness <————————————**X**—> Leniency

Autonomy<—**X**————————————> Control

- ## Responsive parents:
accepting, firm, supportive of autonomy

Acceptance <—**X**————————————> Rejectance

Firmness <—**X**————————————> Leniency

Autonomy<—**X**————————————> Control

HOW PARENTS MAKE A DIFFERENCE

Research shows that the best predictor of a student's achievement in school is not income or social status, but:

1. A home environment that encourages learning.

2. High (but not unrealistic) expectations by parents and caregivers for their children's achievement and future careers.

3. Involvement of parents/caregivers in children's education at school and in the community.

When one or more of the above three conditions are in place, the following results occur:

Higher grades and test scores

Better attendance and more homework done

Fewer placements in special education

More positive attitudes and behavior

Higher graduation rates

Greater enrollment in higher education

WHAT PARENTS CAN DO
TO MAKE A DIFFERENCE

Home Environment. A supportive and stable home environment has great benefits for a child's academic success. Things you can do that research has shown to make a difference:

> Provide time and a quiet place to study.
> Assign responsibility for household chores.
> Be firm about times to get up and go to bed.
> Have dinner together.
> Set limits on TV watching.
> Check up on children when parents are not home.
> Arrange for after-school activities and supervised care.
> Maintain a warm and supportive home.
> Get children ready for school every morning.
> Establish a daily family routine.

Modeling. Parents and other adult caregivers influence children through their own behavior. Things you can do that research has shown to make a difference:

> Communicate through questioning and conversation.
> Use reference materials and the library.
> Discuss the day over dinner.
> Tell stories and share problems.
> Write letters, lists, and messages.

Education beyond Schooling. Much learning takes place outside of school. This learning has been shown to have a key positive impact on school performance. Things you can do that research has shown to make a difference:

> Read to your children.
> Listen to children read.
> Talk about what is being read.
> Enroll your child in sports programs and music lessons.
> Recognize and encourage special talents.
> Use community services, such as Boys and Girls clubs,
>   libraries, the "Y."
> Expose your child to many learning opportunities outside
>   of school, such as visiting museums and nature centers,
>   going to concerts, and talking about current events.
> Listen to and talk with your child about things that are
>   important to you both.

Support and Expectations. Student success is closely related to teacher and parent expectations that are both challenging and realistic. Children also need to have their achievements recognized. Things you can do that make a difference:

> Demonstrate that achievement comes from working hard.
> Set goals and standards that are appropriate for children's age and maturity.
> Inform friends and family about your child's successes.
> Discuss the value of a good education and possible career options.
> Introduce children to role models and mentors.
> Have high expectations for your child's performance at school.
> Have high expectations for your child's later life choices regarding education after high school and career choices.

Engage in Academic Matters. Parents and caregivers who keep in touch with what is going on at school can have an enormous positive impact, both on student attitudes/achievement and on the actual quality of the school. Among many ways to make this a strong connection, you can:

> Show interest in children's progress at school.
> Help with homework.
> Stay in touch with teachers and school staff.
> Respect/understand a teacher's role in your child's education as well as your own role.
> Talk directly with your child's teacher about concerns you might have.
> Talk with the teacher to share what your joint expectations for your child's growth and progress are.
> Give spelling or math drills.
> Visit the classroom.
> Volunteer at the school.
> Share your knowledge with your child's class (your job, a skill or interest you have).
> Help with tutorial and remedial work (your own child's or others').
> Work with small groups or individuals in the classroom.

Support Teacher/School. Even a small amount of assistance can make an enormous difference to the teacher and to the educational experience your child and all the children in the class receive. You can:

> Assist teachers by obtaining and preparing class materials.
> Serve on collaborative decision-making committees.
> Operate a telephone network with other parents.
> Serve as part of a resource pool at your school.
> Help with field trips/assist with extracurricular activities.
> Raise money for school projects.
> Explain school programs and needs to the community.

20 Ways to Support Your Children and Their School

Parents have asked how they can support their children's teachers in doing the best job they can for their students. Here are 20 helpful ways that can show your support.

1. Talk positively about the school experience. Even if your own school memories were not always pleasant, you can help your child by emphasizing the positive opportunity that school affords him. Rather than "You have to go to school today," you might try "You get to go to school today."

2. Talk positively about teachers, education, and homework. Your positive attitude can help your child develop a positive approach to school.

3. Show interest in what your child is learning. By asking questions and letting your child share, you communicate that learning is important and stimulating. Again, emphasize the positive. Rather than ask the standard "What did you do in school today?" try some variations, such as, "What did you do that you really liked?"; "What did you feel good about?"; "What would you like to learn more about?"; "What are you reading?"

4. Continue learning. Your child sees you as a model for many things. If you continue to expand your own knowledge and skills by reading or perhaps even taking a course, your child sees the value in learning.

5. Let your child teach you. As someone once said, "To teach is to learn twice." You can strengthen your child's learning by letting her explain new concepts to you.

6. Help your child find ways to apply his learning to everyday life. The more practical information seems to be, the more motivated your child will be to tackle new material.

7. Avoid the grade trap. While grades are useful in assessing how much your child is learning, it is the learning, not the grades, that is our goal. Avoid the trap of making grades a competition. Help your child learn to relax and enjoy learning without the pressure to compete.

8. Avoid comparing your child's grades with others. Such comparisons are almost always discouraging and counterproductive. It is much better to compare your child's grades with her own grades from the previous report card. "Where have you improved?" "Where do you want to improve more?" "How will you accomplish this?" "How can I help?"

9. Develop realistic expectations for your child. Encourage your child to do the best he can in school, keeping in mind that children will naturally do better in some areas than in others. Also keep in mind that your child is special because of who he is, not how he performs.

10. Provide a quiet place and time for homework. Most students do best with a regular study time that they have agreed upon with their parents. Having a special place for homework, whether it's a quiet desk in their own rooms or at the kitchen table, helps build a routine and atmosphere conducive to work. This can't be accomplished in front of the TV.

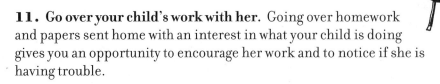

11. Go over your child's work with her. Going over homework and papers sent home with an interest in what your child is doing gives you an opportunity to encourage her work and to notice if she is having trouble.

12. Be a homework consultant, not a tutor. Homework is your child's work, not yours. We recommend that you not sit by your child in an attempt to make sure everything is answered correctly. Mistakes on homework are one way your child's teacher learns what concepts need more explanation. Instead, act as a consultant, being available to offer support and help when your child asks.

13. Encourage your child to read at home. Since reading is the cornerstone of much learning, the more your child practices this essential skill, the better he will do in all his subjects. To maintain the motivation and enjoyment of reading, let your child choose what he wants to read. Easy books, magazines, even comic books as a last resort—anything but material that's "not for children"—should be encouraged.

14. Develop a consistent and effective discipline plan. Using parenting methods that teach your child responsibility, cooperation, and self-esteem will also help your child do well in the classroom. You can avoid being too strict or too lax by taking a parent education course or reading some recommended books.

15. Support the school's discipline plan. A school, like a family, must maintain a certain level of order and structure so that all our children can feel safe and able to learn. If your child is disciplined at school, please help your child learn from the experience by backing up the school at home. If you have a problem with the plan, please bring it up with the administration.

16. Check out disturbing reports. Teachers, as well as parents and students, are not perfect. They may make mistakes. However, if your child shares with you something her teacher did that she felt was grossly unfair or unkind, listen respectfully but don't assume it was as bad as it sounds. Children sometimes exaggerate when their feelings are hurt. If you are disturbed by the situation, call the teacher and check it out. A concerned tone of voice, rather than a hostile or angry tone, will help.

17. Bring a solution as well as a problem. If you have a concern or see a problem you think needs correcting and you bring it to the attention of your child's teacher, also bring a supportive attitude and an idea for a solution. This will help build a cooperative, problem-solving relationship.

18. Be careful about misinformation and gossip. The school "grapevine" can produce a lot of useful information, but it can also become a version of the old game "telephone," where messages become more and more distorted. You can show your support by checking out such information with your child's teacher or the administration. Please call ahead to set up a meeting rather than dropping by for a "quick conference." Your concerns are important to the school and deserve not to be rushed.

19. Come to class meetings when you are invited. These meetings not only provide you with important information, but your attendance also communicates to your child that he and the school are important.

20. Let the school know what is going on at home. When families go through extra stress such as an illness, a death, or a divorce, it can affect the children the most. Please let your child's teacher know about such circumstances. She can often help. In addition, informing the teacher will alert her to possible changes in your child's behavior.

Reprinted with permission from: *Helping Your Child Succeed in School: A Guide for Parents of 4 to 14 Year Olds,* by Popkin, Youngs, and Healy, Active Parenting Publishers, Atlanta, Georgia, 1995. Refer to this excellent resource for more in-depth information.

FOUR COMMON WAYS PARENTS DISCOURAGE THEIR CHILDREN

Focusing on Mistakes

It is easy for us to look at a piece of homework and ignore the thoughtful ideas and amount of effort a child put into it. But we *do* notice the three misspelled words. Often the first thing we do is point out the errors. If we are not also careful to comment upon the things that were done well, then soon a child comes to think she does more wrong than right. Such discouragement leads to more mistakes, which produce more criticism from the parent and so on. Children need to be corrected when they make mistakes. Correction helps them know what to do differently next time. But they probably need to hear four to five times as much about what they do right to balance the effect our criticism may have on their courage and self-esteem.

Personality Attacks and Perfectionism

When we call our children names, such as "lazy," "careless," or "stupid," we are attacking their self-esteem and courage at their core. Not to mention that such tactics usually backfire. After all, if you tell a child that he is lazy, then what should you expect in the future but lazy behavior? Instead focus your comments on the problem behavior. Don't say "Why are you so lazy?"; say instead, "You haven't done your homework."

A subtle form of personality attack is perfectionism. This is the tendency always to require more from the child than she is giving. The message of perfectionism is that no matter how well you do, you should have done better. When children come to believe that they are never quite good enough, they lose motivation: "I never did it well enough anyway, so why try?" Even when these children seem to keep trying, they never feel secure in their achievements. They may get all A's but rather than enjoying the accomplishment, they are already worrying about the next challenge to their perfection. Such perfectionist thinking has been linked to eating disorders and depression in adolescents.

Negative Expectations

In a classic psychology experiment, teachers were told that half the students in their classes had tested high on a measure predicting academic success, and the other half had tested low. In fact, the students were randomly assigned to the two groups, regardless of academic abilities. At the end of the semester, guess which group had the better grades? The group the teachers thought would do better actually did do better. Conversely, the teachers' negative expectations for the other group was a significant factor in the group's poor showing. Negative expectations from teachers and parents discourage children from trying.

Our children can sense when we expect the worst from them, even if we don't use the words. If you believe your child is hopeless in math you can say, "I know you can do this," but your tone of voice will give a different message. Or perhaps you wait only a few seconds for your child to answer a question and then hurriedly give him the answer. You and your child may not even be consciously aware of this difference, but the message is received: "You don't think I can get it."

Overprotection

When we step in and do for children what they could eventually do for themselves, we send the message that "you can't handle it." Children must be free to overcome their frustrations, solve their own problems, and accept the consequences of their choices if they are to develop the stamina required to succeed in school and in the community. The overprotected child easily gives up when things are difficult. She is quick to shout, "it's not fair" at the slightest transgression. She looks for someone else to solve her problems and lives with many unrealistic fears that hamper her growth.

Think of the problems such attitudes cause in the classroom, where teachers cope with 25 or more students and must rely on a degree of independence from each one. An overprotected child who expects special treatment at school is in for a frustrating, discouraging time.

How can a parent tell when she is offering reasonable protection and when she is overprotecting? Two rules of thumb may help:

1. Ask yourself what is the worst that could happen if you don't step in.
2. Never do for your child on a regular basis what your child can do for herself. Be on guard against the rationalization, "But it's easier to do it myself." It may be easier and faster in the short run but think of the damage you do in the long run. Eventually your child may not be able to DO much of anything for himself, including school work, that presents a challenge.

Modified and adapted with permission from: *Helping Your Child Succeed in School: A Guide for Parents of 4 to 14 Year Olds*, by Popkin, Youngs, and Healy, Active Parenting Publishers, Atlanta, Georgia, 1995. Refer to this excellent resource for more in-depth information.

TURNING DISCOURAGEMENT INTO ENCOURAGEMENT

Avoiding the tendency to discourage our children is a major step in the right direction. The next step is to look for opportunities to actively encourage them. We can use the power of encouragement in general ways to build a bedrock of courage and self-esteem, and we can use it in specific ways to encourage positive behavior, values, and attitudes.

Instead of...
focusing on mistakes————————> build on strengths
expecting too much—perfectionism——> show acceptance
negative expectations————————> show confidence
expecting too little—overprotection——> stimulate independence

Build on Strengths

Our successes bolster our courage and motivate us to want to do even better. The same is true for our children. Helping them experience the joy of achievement and then commenting on the strengths they called upon to make achievement happen is a wonderful way to encourage further progress.

1. Focus your encouragement on the behavior rather than the child.
Parents sometimes ask what is wrong with telling a child that she is a "good girl," or otherwise praising her personality. Children experience such praise as a double-edged sword: "I am a 'good' girl when I do what you want; therefore, I must be a 'bad' girl when I don't."

2. Comment on the effort, not just the results.

NO: Not saying anything until the report card arrives.

YES: Giving encouragement throughout the year: "You are really working hard on your reading. I can hear the improvement."

3. Break large tasks into smaller steps.

NO: "Let's organize your room today."

YES: "Let's organize your closet today."

Later: "You did a great job with the closet! Doesn't it look terrific? How about making a date to tackle the bookshelf next?"

4. Look for past examples of strengths to encourage your child to take the next step.

NO: "I know you can do this report."

YES: "You did a good job writing that paper on Eleanor Roosevelt. I know this report is a little longer, but I'll bet if you break it down into sections, you'll do a fine job."

Show Acceptance

Parents who are achievers sometimes unwittingly send the message that they accept their children *as long as they perform to their parents' standards.* Because all children have a fundamental need to belong, to feel accepted and wanted—especially by their parents—any suspicion that Mom's or Dad's acceptance is conditional undermines children's sense of security, self-esteem, and courage. We must let our children know through our words and actions that we love and value them for themselves—just because they are our children. Our acceptance is free and unconditional. Sure, we want to encourage their success, and we do not accept certain behavior as okay, but we always accept them as unique and special human beings who are gifts in our lives.

"I really enjoy being with you."

"I can tell it's you from hearing that great laugh of yours."

"I know you're disappointed in not making the team, but you tried your best, and that's what's important."

"I'm glad you are my daughter."

Show Confidence

All children can learn, even though some may take longer than others to master a concept or a skill. Your confidence in your child's ability to keep going when he feels frustration and defeat, your confidence that he will eventually succeed, your confidence that he will make something useful of his life—this is the encouragement that can make the difference between success and failure.

To show confidence, you really have to believe that your child is capable of success. If you don't believe in her, then she has to overcome your doubts as well as her own. That's an uphill battle. Some tips:

1. Keep your confidence in line with reality. Just as it's silly to have confidence that you'll win the lottery, you don't want to set up false or unrealistic expectations by showing confidence that your child will make all As when he has been struggling to pass.

> NO: "I know you're failing this course, but I believe you can get an A if you really try."

> YES: "I know you can pass this course if you give it the same effort you give your rollerblading."

2. Show confidence by giving responsibility. Allowing children to take on additional responsibilities is an excellent way to communicate your confidence. Keep the level of responsibility in line with their age and ability to handle it, then look for opportunities to encourage their efforts.

> "We can get a pet hamster if you will feed it and clean out the cage."

> "I think you are old enough to help me with some of the house chores. Would you rather start by learning how to use the vacuum cleaner or the furniture polish?"

3. Ask your child's opinion. This communicates that you have confidence in her ability to think.

> " You've been studying about World War II. Do you think that was a war worth fighting?"

> "Where do you think we should go on our picnic? The park or the nature center?"

4. Don't rescue your children from frustration. When children have difficulty with a task that we can easily do, it is very tempting to step in and take over. Instead, when they become frustrated, try offering partial help and let them still take part of the credit. If you think they can complete the task by themselves if they keep trying, you might simply offer encouragement.

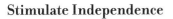

"You can do it. Keep at it."

"Come on, just a little more and you'll have it."

"Here, let me help you pull the bow through. Now you pull it tight. Great!"

Stimulate Independence

As children learn to do more and more for themselves, they become more confident, take on new challenges, learn more, and continue to succeed. By stimulating our children's independence, we can help them grow into mature, responsible adults.

"Now that we've gone over the steps in order, I think you can do this project on your own. I'm looking forward to seeing it when you're finished."

"From now on I'd like each of us to make his own bed before coming down for breakfast."

More Encouragement Tips

As you look for ways to encourage each of your children, keep in mind that what one child finds encouraging, another may find discouraging. Observe what words or actions each of your children best responds to. Make sure that you:

• **Make the encouragement immediate.** The sooner your encouragement follows the attitude or behavior you approve, the more powerful it is.

• **Make the encouragement genuine.** If you tell your child she is doing well when she knows she isn't, your credibility isn't worth much. Future encouragement may be doubted, even when it's sincere.

• **Make the encouragement specific.** Specific positive feedback tells your children what to keep doing in the future. This promotes both motivation and improvement: "I like the way you used gray in the sky. It makes the castle look more gloomy."

What Encouragement Sounds Like

You can use hundreds of words and phrases to actively encourage your children. Find the ones that suit your style and please your children's ears. Here are some ideas:

attagirl	awesome	way to go
nice job	I really like that	you can do it
now you're getting it	great	terrific
super	neat	cool
attaboy	amazing	thanks
I appreciate it	you got it	you made it
you did it	superb	wonderful
bingo	now you're cooking	keep it up
that's the way	I'm proud of you	you must feel proud
you really earned it	good for you	gimme five
wow!	good effort	nice try
try again, you can do it	how special!	very good

Modified and adapted with permission from: *Helping Your Child Succeed in School: A Guide for Parents of 4 to 14 Year Olds*, by Popkin, Youngs, and Healy, Active Parenting Publishers, Atlanta, Georgia, 1995. Refer to this excellent resource for more in-depth information.

BUILDING A STRONG MATH/SCIENCE FOUNDATION AT HOME

First, help children of any age become good problem solvers. Here are some tips:

1. Encourage questions, particularly those which have more than one possible answer, and preferably ones to which you don't know the answer. ("I'm not sure why leaves have different shapes—let's collect some and try to figure out some reasons.")

2. Ask open-ended questions and welcome innovative responses. ("What do you think these woods will look like a hundred years from now?" "What would children do if there weren't any schools and everyone stayed home and learned from a computer?")

3. Encourage divergent approaches to everyday situations, within reason. (If your child can think of a reason for setting the table in a new and different way, why not?)

4. Help your child to tolerate some uncertainty—effective thinkers can delay the best solution to a problem until they have tried out several hypotheses.

5. Provide toys and games that encourage a variety of types of play which the youngster must create himself; praise and admire innovative uses of play construction, or game materials.

6. Show your child how to estimate. ("You have nine pennies in your bank—that's close to a dime." "We have to drive 295 miles to Grandmother's house—that's almost 300 miles.")

7. Practice "guess and test." ("I'm not sure what will happen if we put lemonade in the Jell-O instead of water—let's guess some possibilities and then see what happens.")

8. Avoid using the words "right" and "wrong" unless a moral or safety issue is at stake; take time to listen to the child's ideas before passing judgment. Try out the phrase "That's an interesting idea—tell me more."

9. Work hard on helping your child feel secure enough to take sensible risks.

Practical Math and Science Learning at Home

Next, try some family activities to build numerical and scientific concepts:

1. Cooking offers a wealth of possibilities for understanding the important ideas of quantity, measuring, sequencing steps in a problem, following directions accurately, fractions, and testing hypotheses. Here is an enjoyable, meaningful, and delicious learning experience!

2. Family games involving cards, numbers, or money promote an understanding of relative quantity and build computational skills. Games requiring visual organization or strategy are also valuable.

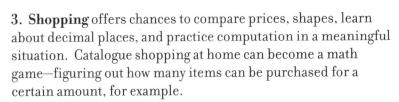

3. Shopping offers chances to compare prices, shapes, learn about decimal places, and practice computation in a meaningful situation. Catalogue shopping at home can become a math game—figuring out how many items can be purchased for a certain amount, for example.

4. Every school-age child should have some sort of **allowance** to manage, however small, and real experience buying small items and getting change. Older children can learn about interest in a natural context from a bank or if they need to borrow from the parental exchequer.

5. Travel games, such as license plate bingo, keeping mileage records, or even computing gas mileage can be fun. Working with maps builds graphing and directional skills and can make a child feel very important.

6. Collecting inspires many budding scientists, and **exploring nature** with an interested adult has kindled the interest of many future biologists.

7. Measuring and weighing activities are appropriate even for young children. Making diagrams of rooms in the house or maps of the yard or neighborhood is fun. You might try introducing nonstandard measurements, such as "How many Daddy-shoe-lengths wide is the kitchen?" *The Guinness Book of World Records* is a rich source of relative measurements.

8. Using time is the best way to learn about it. Relate time to events that are meaningful for the child and use appropriate terms ("What are we doing now?"; "What will we do *after/while* we eat lunch?"). Pasting or drawing pictures of activities on a daily calendar while discussing past and upcoming events makes "then" and "soon" more understandable than using abstract concepts of days, weeks, months, or seasons.

9. Following directions is one of the most important skills from the home. Taking steps in order, planning ahead, and talking about what to do before tackling the task can all be encouraged. Cooking, as noted earlier, treasure hunts, and building models are all sequential step-following activities. For older children, map and compass skills are very helpful.

10. Calculator games are a good source of problem-solving situations with numerical concepts.

These are only a few of the multitude of activities which are the natural base of math and science learning. They are essentially about the real world, which is the best place to learn about them.

Troubleshooting Problems in Math and Science

1. Watch for multiple danger signs (listed below) that persist for several months. Many students experience temporary "glitches" in the learning process, so exercise reasonable patience and help the child try to work the problem out. (For younger children, you many need to take action more promptly than for older ones.) Danger signs:

- confusion about math or science homework

- frequently writing numerals backwards or confusing plus and minus signs after age seven or eight

- tears or stomachaches on test days

- persistent difficulty learning "facts" (addition, subtraction, multiplication tables)

- trouble estimating (gives far-fetched answer to story problems)

2. Keep a folder of papers that document the child's difficulty.

3. Schedule a conference with the teacher. Discuss the child's papers you have saved. Find out if special help is available at school. If necessary, ask to speak to the school psychologist or learning specialist.

4. If the school has not been using manipulatives in teaching mathematics (concrete objects such as blocks, rods, or geometric forms that teach number concepts), ask if this could happen or if some trained person could use them to work with your child during free time or after school. For older students, teachers usually offer extra help periods. Expect your child to sign up (and show up) for any extra help that is offered.

5. If the school has not been using hands-on materials in teaching science (real objects and substances), ask if this could happen. Just reading about science is not adequate. In the short run, ask that a materials-based science program be offered after school.

6. If outside help is your only recourse, look for a clinic or experienced tutor who will use many different approaches other than worksheets to get the concepts across.

The "Practical Math and Science Learning at Home" section is reprinted with permission from: *Helping Your Child Succeed in School: A Guide for Parents of 4 to 14 Year Olds*, by Popkin, Youngs, and Healy, Active Parenting Publishers, Atlanta, Georgia, 1995. Based on material in "Practical Learning," from *Your Child's Growing Mind*, by Jane M. Healy, Doubleday, Inc., New York, 1994.

The "Troubleshooting Problems in Math and Science" section is modified and adapted with permission from: *Helping Your Child Succeed in School: A Guide for Parents of 4 to 14 Year Olds*, by Popkin, Youngs, and Healy, Active Parenting Publishers, Atlanta, Georgia, 1995. Refer to this excellent resource for more in-depth information.

CHARACTERISTICS OF PARENTING THAT PROMOTE ACADEMIC SUCCESS

The following three approaches to parenting are key to promoting academic success in children. While all parents fall somewhere between the extremes, research strongly indicates that parents who are closer to acceptance, firmness, and autonomy have children who are more successful in school.

Acceptance <————————————> Rejectance

Accepting parents are affectionate, frequent in their praise, involved in their child's life, and responsive to their child's emotional needs.

Children raised by accepting parents feel that they can turn to their parents when they have problems, that their parents encourage them, that their parents enjoy spending time with them, and that their parents are dependable sources of guidance or assistance.

Firmness <————————————> Leniency

Firm parents have clear rules that the child is expected to follow and they set clear expectations that the child will behave in a mature and responsible fashion. They are consistent.

Children raised by firm parents know what their parents expect of them and know that there are consequences for violating their expectations.

Autonomy <————————————> Control

Parents who support autonomy in their children tolerate and encourage their child's sense of individuality. They encourage their child to express himself or herself and enjoy watching their child develop into a separate and autonomous individual.

Children raised to be autonomous feel that self-expression is a valued trait, and that their parents' love and respect for them is not contingent on having the same opinions and ideas as their parents. They know that it is important for a person to speak up for what he or she believes.

Based on: *Beyond the Classroom: Why School Reform has Failed and What Parents Need To Do*, Laurence Steinberg, Simon & Schuster, New York, 1996.

RECOMMENDED FAMILY EDUCATION PROGRAMS

Family Math

The basic goal of **FAMILY MATH** is to promote parents as effective partners in helping their children succeed in mathematics. Hands-on, problem-solving activities are used to illustrate math concepts that reinforce the school curriculum and demonstrate the importance of mathematics for future work and education. FAMILY MATH transforms student attitudes toward mathematics, gives parents a sense of confidence, re-energizes teachers, and builds community. The program has reached over a million adults and children from diverse communities all over the United States and the world. Evolving from and part of the Lawrence Hall of Science EQUALS program, FAMILY MATH is designed to promote equity and make math accessible to all students regardless of race, gender, or class. The *Family Math* book has been a bestseller since its publication. There is a national network of FAMILY MATH workshop presenters who prepare leaders for family classes. Class sessions introduce families to activities that can be repeated at home using common household materials. They include math activities and math-related career information and role models. A typical series consists of four to eight weekly classes of one or two hours. For more information on setting up or participating in a program, or to obtain the *Family Math* book in English or Spanish, contact: FAMILY MATH at the Lawrence Hall of Science, University of California, Berkeley, CA 94720-5200, call (510) 642-1823 or visit http://www.lhs.berkeley.edu/EQUALS/

Family Science

Family Science is an informal science education program that gives parents and children opportunities to work and learn together. Hands-on activities that use easy-to-find, inexpensive materials encourage families to explore concepts and see the role science plays in daily life. The Lawrence Hall of Science (LHS) is one of the original Family Science sites and leadership training workshops can be arranged through the EQUALS program. For information about the recently-published book *Family Science*, contact David Heil and Associates in Portland, Oregon, at (503) 245-2102.

Active Parenting Publishers and Videos

Active Parenting Publishers delivers research-based quality education programs for parents, children, and teachers to schools, hospitals, social services organizations, churches, and industry. Their excellent book *Helping Your Child Succeed in School* is the source for a number of the parent handouts in this GEMS Parent Partners program. Founded by noted family therapist Michael H. Popkin, Ph.D., and based in Marietta, Georgia (near Atlanta), Active Parenting Publishers assists parents and professionals seeking innovative resources in parent education. After three years of research to arrive at effective ways to integrate video and group discussion, in 1983 they produced the first video-based parent education program, the Active Parenting Discussion Program, in six two-hour sessions. Revised as Active Parenting Today, it is their most popular program. They feature many other video discussion programs and publications, including Active Parenting of Teens; Active Teaching: Enhancing Discipline, Self-Esteem and Student Performance; Free the Horses: A Self-Esteem Adventure; Healing and Helping through Loss; Parents on Board; and 1,2,3,4 Parents!: Parenting Children Ages 1-4. They also focus on current issues, such as drug abuse and school violence. Active Parenting Publishers has been awarded the Positive Parenting Award from the National Council for Children's Rights. For more information, call (800) 825-0060, e-mail cservice@activeparenting.com or visit their web site at http://www.activeparenting.com/

Session 1: Research References

Becher, Rhoda McShane, *Parent Involvement: A Review of Research and Principles of Successful Practice*, National Institute of Education, 1984.

Bermudez, Andrea B., Rakow, Steven J., (Principal Investigators), *Critical Issues in Parental Involvement*, Research Center for Language and Culture, University of Houston-Clear Lake, 1992.

Bradley, B., "How to Raise Smart Kids," *Parenting*, 66–71, September, 1993.

"Bring Out the Scientist in Your Child," *PTA Today*, 17(5), 13–15, March, 1992.

Campbell, P. B., *Math, Science, and Your Daughter: What Can Parents Do?* U.S. Department of Education, Washington, DC, 1992.

Carrasquillo, A. L., London, C. B. G., *Parents and Schools: A Source Book*, Garland Publishing, New York, 1993.

* Clark, Reginald M., "Homework-Focused Parenting Practices that Positively Affect Student Achievement," in *Families and Schools in a Pluralistic Society*, Nancy Feyl Chavkin, editor, Chapter 4, 85–105, State University of New York Press, Albany, 1993.

Clark, Reginald M., "Why Disadvantaged Students Succeed: What Happens Outside School is Critical," Public Welfare, Spring 1990, 17–23, 1990.

Dauber, Susan, Epstein, Joyce, "Parent Attitudes and Practices of Involvement in Inner-City Elementary and Middle Schools," in *Families and Schools in a Pluralistic Society*, Nancy Feyl Chavkin, editor, Chapter 2, 53–71, State University of New York Press, Albany, 1993.

Epstein, Joyce L., "Effects on Student Achievement of Teachers' Practices of Parent Involvement," *Advances in Reading/Language Research*, Volume 5, 261–276, JAI Press, Greenwich, Connecticut, 1991.

"Get Into the Equation: Math and Science, Parents and Children," College Board, New York, 1987.

* Henderson, Anne T., Berla, Nancy (editors), *A New Generation of Evidence: The Family Is Critical to Student Achievement*, Center for Law and Education, Washington, DC, 1997.

Howley, C., "The World According to Science: Think About It," ERIC Clearinghouse on Rural Education and Small Schools, Charleston, West Virginia, 1991.

* Hrabowski, Freeman A., Maton, Kennith I., Greif, Geoffrey L., *Beating the Odds: Raising Academically Successful African American Males*, Oxford University Press, New York, 1998.

Irvine, David J., *Parent Involvement Affects Children's Cognitive Growth*, University of the State of New York, State Education Department, Division of Research, Albany, August, 1979.

Kellaghan, Thomas, Sloane, Kathryn, Alvarez, Benjamin, Bloom, Benjamin, *The Home Environment and School Learning: Promoting Parent Involvement in the Education of Children*, Jossey-Bass, Inc., San Francisco, 1993.

* Kirshbaum, Roberta (with Robin Dellabough), *Parent Power: 90 Winning Ways to Be Involved and Help Your Child Get the Most Out of School*, Hyperion, New York, 1998.

Lara, A., "Homework: How to End the Struggle," *Parenting,* 124–131, September, 1993.

Paulu, N., *Helping Your Child Learn Science*, Office of Educational Research and Improvement, Washington, DC, 1992.

* Popkin, Michael H., Youngs, Bettie B., Healy, Jane M., *Helping Your Child Succeed in School: A Guide for Parents of 4 to 14 Year Olds*, Active Parenting Publishers, Atlanta, Georgia, 1995.

Simich-Dudgeon, Carmen, "Increasing Student Achievement through Teacher Knowledge About Parent Involvement," in *Families and Schools in a Pluralistic Society*, Nancy Feyl Chavkin, editor, Chapter 10, 189–204, State University of New York Press, Albany, 1993.

Snow, Catharine E., Barnes, Wendy S., Chandler, Jean, Goodman, Irene F., Hemphill, Lowry, *Unfulfilled Expectations: Home and School Influences on Literacy*, Harvard University Press, Cambridge, 1991.

* Steinberg, Laurence, *Beyond the Classroom: Why School Reform has Failed and What Parents Need To Do,* Touchstone, New York, 1997.

Stevenson, David L., Baker, David P., "The Family-School Relation and the Child's School Performance," *Child Development*, Volume 58, 1348–1357, 1987.

Walberg, Herbert J., "Families as Partners in Educational Productivity," *Phi Beta Kappan*, 397–400, February, 1984.

Ziegler, Suzanne, *The Effects of Parent Involvement on Children's Achievement: The Significance of Home/School Links*, Toronto Board of Education, Ontario, Canada, October, 1987.

Engaging Messages—Session 1

The following short digests share research findings related to the information presented in Session 1: How Parents Make a Difference. These are best used *after* Session 1 has been presented. Some schools put one engaging message in each weekly bulletin. Parents come to expect and look forward to learning something about what research studies have found. Other schools promote attendance at future sessions by sharing some of what was learned at the previous session. Even if you don't present Session 1, these engaging messages can be successfully used.

Families Whose Children Do Well in School

Research studies find that the home life of families whose children do well in school often includes:

- Expressing high but realistic expectations for achievement;
- Encouraging children's development and progress in school;
- Establishing a daily family routine;
- Monitoring out-of-school activities;
- Modeling the values of learning, self-discipline, and hard work;
- Reading, writing, and discussions among family members;
- Using community resources for family needs.

The above qualities of home life are of major importance. It is often assumed that parents' level of education or parents' understanding of math and science play a major role. However, research studies suggest that these are not key factors.

How Parents React to Academic Success or Failure is Important

When parents communicate to children that their academic successes (both small and large) are due to hard work and diligence and their academic difficulties are due to not working hard enough, it leads students to conclude that **they** control their scholastic fate, not their teachers, their genes, or the luck of the draw.

Schools Improve When Parents Get Involved

Research studies show that parent involvement greatly improves the overall quality of schools. Schools that find ways to work well with families have:

- Higher student achievement;
- Improved teacher morale;
- Higher ratings of teachers by parents;
- More support from families;
- Better reputations in the community.

This has been shown to be the case in both low and high resource communities.

The Importance of How Parents and Teachers Relate

Children's attitudes and performance in school increases when parents and teachers:

- understand and respect each other;
- share similar expectations; and
- stay in communication.

Talking directly with the teacher about concerns you might have creates a relationship of open communication and mutual respect. Children who conclude "my parent and my teacher are working this out together" will be more successful than children who conclude "my parent doesn't like my teacher/school."

Parents can cause confusion or undermine a child's success when they communicate negative impressions of a teacher or school to their child.

Families Whose Children "Get Ahead" in Life

Some research studies have identified two types of families—those that produced students who tended to "get ahead" and those that produced students who tended to just "get by." According to these studies, "getting by" families tend to choose to maintain their way of life rather than focusing on rising higher on the socioeconomic ladder. For example, children in such families may be encouraged to finish high school but not to attend college.

"Getting ahead" families stressed high grades, paid attention to what was happening at school, suggested options for education after high school, and discussed possible future occupations.

When Parents Volunteer in the Classroom

Students develop better attitudes toward their school and school work when their parents are involved with the school's instructional program.

This effect has been found to carry over to benefit all students, not just those whose parents volunteered in the classroom. For instance, a large research study found all students placed higher value on their school work when parents served as classroom aides (as compared to non-parent aides).

Parent volunteers in the classroom have many other positive benefits. The teacher and parents involved get to know each other better and parents become much more aware of the teacher's approach and the realities of the classroom.

When it comes to math and science, the extra help several parent volunteers can provide can make the difference in being able to provide active instruction. Activity-based math and science have been shown to be more educationally effective than more passive forms of instruction.

Parents: Be Accepting, Be Firm, Support your Child's Autonomy

Research shows that parents who approach parenting in these ways have children who succeed in school.

Accepting parents are affectionate, frequent in their praise, involved in their child's life, and responsive to their child's emotional needs. Children raised by accepting parents feel that they can turn to their parents when they have problems, that their parents encourage them, that their parents enjoy spending time with them, and that their parents are dependable sources of guidance or assistance.

Firm parents have clear rules that the child is expected to follow and they set clear expectations that the child will behave in a mature and responsible fashion. They are consistent. Children raised by firm parents know what their parents expect of them and know that there are consequences for violating their expectations.

Parents who support autonomy in their children tolerate and encourage their child's sense of individuality. They encourage their child to express himself or herself and enjoy watching their child develop into a separate and autonomous individual. Children raised to be autonomous feel that self-expression is a valued trait, and that their parents' love and respect for them is not contingent on having the same opinions and ideas as their parents. They know that it is important for a person to speak up for what he or she believes.

Session 2: How Students Learn Best

Overview

This workshop gives participants the opportunity to quickly experience several teaching approaches, including free exploration, reading a text, and more structured investigation and application. The experience is used to launch a discussion of the ways that children learn best and to highlight the need for a healthy balance of different teaching modalities in the classroom and at home. In the second part of the session, participants are introduced to the idea of multiple intelligences, as one way to think about the rich range of potential capabilities of their children, in order to help them gain increased success.

The session begins with participants doing a structured activity in which they add an exact amount of water to a few small piles of a mysterious powdered substance. They watch in amazement as the powder transforms into an ever-expanding gooey mass with each drop of water that is added. As a group, they are challenged to do further open-ended explorations using two new liquids. They then read a brief written article describing the chemistry of the substance and answer questions based on what they've read. Finally they are challenged to apply their knowledge and invent a use for the substance in a "real-world" context. Before sharing their responses with the whole group, they discuss their reactions to each part of the activity within their table groups. This allows them to reflect a bit on their experiences and express themselves first in a smaller, safer arena. It also serves to help focus the larger group discussion on how various methods can be used to help students learn. The presenter then summarizes for the participants what educational research says about how students learn. Participants also receive a concise, jargon-free handout on the topic to refer to and digest at a later time. The presenter poses the question of how parents can help to encourage this kind of learning at home. Another handout, The Art of the Question is provided to further assist parents in encouraging their children's learning.

In the second part of this session, the presenter provides an introduction to the fascinating and influential theory of multiple intelligences. This idea, first articulated by Harvard Professor Howard Gardner and since applied in many educational settings, expands the concept of "intelligence" from the linguistic and logical abilities that have traditionally been defined as "smart" to include many other human capabilities. To get acquainted with this idea, the workshop participants take a personal "inventory" of some of their own aptitudes and inclinations as they learn about seven ways students can demonstrate intelligence: linguistic, logical, musical, spatial, bodily-kinesthetic, interpersonal, and intrapersonal. The emphasis is placed on how parents' awareness of their child's special talents and capabilities can help provide insight into ways to encourage them to succeed in school. We also provide a version of the multiple intelligence inventory which parents may wish to use with their children at home. The take-away messages from the workshop seek to provide practical ways to help parents implement what they've learned about the best ways to educate their child.

Note: There is no optional 10-minute extension for this session.

Extending the impact of this session

This session provides parents with an initial basis for understanding the diversity of approaches used in modern science and mathematics education, especially the emphasis on active learning and, in science education, the central importance of inquiry. The *National Science Education Standards,* for example state that "inquiry into authentic questions is the central strategy for teaching science." In a brief, intriguing way, this is what parents experience in this session as they investigate a unique substance. From their discussion of what they did, they are likely to be more open to a diversity of teaching approaches, and to realize the value of activity-based science. Based on your school's curriculum, you may also want to structure other similar sessions focused on different subject matter, aimed at providing parents with a concrete look at the main goals and approaches of specific programs at your school.

This session can also be an ideal springboard into active parent volunteer involvement in the classroom. Many activity-based science and math activities benefit greatly from parent volunteers, and this session often engenders an awareness by parents of how compelling such activities can be for their children and all students. Parents and other adult caregivers can also gain an awareness of the logistical and material needs of science instruction, and see how an extra pair of adult hands in class, finding ways to obtain materials before class, or helping out with other needed tasks can be a great benefit. Many such tasks can be taken on by parents with a relatively small investment of time and energy. Many teachers in your school or district may already have ongoing programs and mechanisms for parents to volunteer in the classroom or help in other ways—this session can be linked directly to those specific programs. Presenting this session can help spur other teachers to take advantage of the session to recruit new volunteers.

Time Frame

Total Workshop: 75 minutes
    Introduction (5 minutes)
    Experiencing Different Teaching Approaches (25 minutes)
    Debrief of Learning Activities (20 minutes)
    What Research Says About Learning (5 minutes)
    Multiple Intelligences and Different Learning Styles
        (15 minutes)
    Conclusion (5 minutes)

What You Need

For the presenter:

- ❏ 1 each of the following overhead transparencies (masters on pages 95–105):
  - 1. Goals for the Session
  - 2. Structured Activity
  - 3. Open-ended Exploration
  - 4. Read and Answer Activity
  - 5. Problem-solving Challenge
  - 6. Overview of Teaching Approaches
  - 7. Which Teaching Approaches are Best
  - 8. Consider the Goals of the Lesson
  - 9. Reasons Why a Teacher Might Choose a Particular Approach or Sequence of Approaches
  - 10. How Students Learn Best
  - 11. Multiple Intelligences
- ❏ overhead projector
- ❏ blank overhead transparency
- ❏ overhead transparency pen
- ❏ extension cord (optional)
- ❏ 1 vial of PSA (see Getting Ready for information on where to obtain PSA)
- ❏ 1 pint-sized container of sugar
- ❏ 1 pint-sized container of salt
- ❏ 1 quart-sized pitcher (for mixing solutions)
- ❏ 1 mixing spoon
- ❏ masking tape
- ❏ indelible "sharpie" marker for writing on masking tape
- ❏ 1 dishtub
- ❏ 2 sponges (or paper towels)
- ❏ 2 cafeteria trays (or cookie sheets) to carry materials to tables

For each participant:

- ❏ 1 of the following on-table handout:
  - Learning Memories (master on page 106)
- ❏ 1 of each of the following in-session handouts:
  - 1. Information about PSA (master on page 90)
  - 2. Questions to Answer on PSA (master on page 91)
  - 3. Multiple Intelligences Inventory for Adults (master on pages 92–93)
- ❏ 1 of each of the following take-home handouts:
  - 1. How Students Learn Best (master on page 107)
  - 2. Sample Questions to Encourage Learning/The Art of the Question (masters on pages 108 and 109)
  - 3. What Are "Multiple Intelligences?" (master on pages 110–111)
  - 4. Multiple Intelligences and Your Children (master on page 112)
  - 5. Assessing Your Children's Learning Habits (master on pages 113–114)
  - 6. Session 2: Research References (master on pages 115–117)

What is PSA? PSA is a safe powder that is used as an absorbent in a variety of agricultural and personal products. PSA stands for polysodium acrylate. Sometimes it is also referred to as sodium polyacrylate (SPA).

"If I had not experienced how great the mystery powder activity is, I would have been hesitant to go to the trouble of getting it. Parents were intrigued and engaged as they investigated the powder—it made the session a huge success. Be sure to emphasize that ordering it is as easy as making a single phone call."

For each group of 4–6 participants:

❑ 1 small plastic or paper plate (6"– 8") preferably a color other than white (so the white powder will be easy to see on the plate)

❑ 3 cups (10 oz. flexible "Solo" brand plastic cups work well)

❑ 4 medicine droppers (or homemade drinking straw droppers)

❑ 4 stir sticks (wooden coffee stirrers, popsicle sticks, or drinking straws cut in half; one end cut at an angle to probe the gelled PSA)

❑ 1 Debrief Card (master on page 94)

❑ 1 cafeteria tray (or cookie sheet)

Getting Ready

At Least a Week Before the Workshop

Acquire materials. You will need one set of materials for each table of 4–6 participants. All materials can be purchased locally except the PSA. It can be ordered from Flinn Scientific, P.O. Box 219, Batavia, IL 60510, (800-452-1261). It is inexpensive, and a 100 gram bottle will last a long time. PSA can sometimes be purchased locally from floral shops (which may use it to preserve floral arrangements) or nurseries (as a soil amendment).

If you are making homemade droppers (rather than using medicine droppers) you can use straws in the following way. Bend over the top third of the straw and pinch the double part of the straw (not at the fold itself). Keep squeezing as you lower the straw into the liquid. Stop squeezing. Then lift the straw out of the cup. Pinch a little bit at a time to make drops come out.

Before the Day of the Workshop

1. Duplicate handouts. Decide which take-home handouts you would like to make available to participants. For each participant, duplicate one copy of the on-table handout, one copy of each of the three in-session handouts, and whichever of the six take-home handouts you have decided to use. Copy the Sample Questions to Encourage Learning and The Art of the Question handouts back-to-back.

2. Duplicate debrief cards. Duplicate one copy of the Debrief Card for each group of 4–6 participants.

3. Make overhead transparencies. Make one of each of the eleven overhead transparencies.

4. Label cups. Label three cups for each table of 4–6 participants. The cups should say: "Water," "Salt Water," and "Sugar Water."

Immediately Before the Workshop

1. Set up the room. Arrange the room so groups of 4–6 participants can sit at a table together. If you are in a classroom, move desks together to make "tables." Tables should be oriented so all the table groups can join a large group discussion, and see what's projected on the overhead.

2. Set up overhead projector. Set up overhead projector at the front of the room near where you will stand.

3. Have overhead transparencies on hand. Set the blank transparency, the overhead pen, and the 11 overhead transparencies (in numbered order) next to the overhead projector.

4. Set out on-table handout. Place one copy of the handout, Learning Memories at each seat, so parents will have something to look at when they first arrive.

5. Set up a tray of materials for each table group. Set up one tray of materials for each table group in the following way.

   a. Use a tiny scoop (the end of a stir stick or a drinking straw cut at an angle) to place four very small piles of PSA powder on a plate. (The piles should be approximately the size of a pea or even less.)

   b. Fill the plain water cup half full.

   c. Place plates (with PSA piles), water cups, and four medicine droppers on each tray.

Have the trays on hand to distribute. Do not place them at the tables yet.

6. Make salt solution. In the pitcher, add 3 tablespoons of salt to 4 cups water and stir until dissolved. Pour into the cups labeled "Salt Water" (1 for each table group). Place the cups on a tray for distribution later in the session. Rinse out the pitcher.

"I made my salt and sugar solutions by putting a teaspoon of salt (or sugar) in a plastic cup of water, rather than mixing the solutions first in a pitcher." The exact concentration of the solution is not important so this or other "quick and dirty" methods will work.

7. Make sugar solution. In the pitcher, add 3 tablespoons of sugar to 4 cups water and stir until dissolved. Pour into cups labeled "Sugar Water" (1 for each table group). Place the cups on a tray for distribution later in the session.

8. Have in-class handouts ready for distribution. Have Information about PSA, Questions to Answer on PSA, and Multiple Intelligences Inventory for Adults ready to pass out. Also have the Debrief Cards ready to distribute.

9. Have take-home handouts ready for distribution. Have the take-home handouts you've decided to use ready to pass out at the end of the session.

Some parents may be interested in pursuing educational research findings on how students learn best in more detail. A Research Reference list is provided for this and the other two presentations included in this guide. You may want to mention this to parents up front.

Introduction (5 minutes)

1. Introduce yourself. Introduce yourself and the context of the workshop. Tell them that this session for parents is intended to: a) present what research says about the topic of how students learn best; and b) provide a forum for discussion about this important educational topic. While this session was designed from the perspective of mathematics and science, and elementary-aged students, most of what will be presented can be generalized to all of learning.

Point out that an hour and fifteen minutes is not long to accomplish the goals of the workshop, and that you have a tight schedule planned. In order to be able to end on time, you will appreciate their cooperation and attention in the workshop.

2. Learning memories reveal the diversity of students' experiences. Refer to the on-table handout, Learning Memories. Point out that you won't take the time to ask them to share their own memories about learning math and science, but if we did, we would likely uncover a wide range of experiences, like those that are described on the handout. Some of us have great memories of a particular teacher or class; others have painful memories. Most people have a mixture of positive and less-than-positive memories.

Let them know that the point is there are many different teaching approaches and that different students respond differently to those approaches depending on many factors.

3. Outline goals for the day. Show overhead transparency #1.

Goals for the Session

· Consider different teaching approaches and their strengths in helping students learn

· Receive a summary of what research says about how students learn best

· Discuss the theory of "multiple intelligences" and current thinking about different learning styles

· Take home suggestions for you to help your child know more about his/her own learning style to become a more effective learner

---

Explain that the first part of today's session will focus on different **teaching approaches** and their strengths in helping students learn. They will learn some of the rationale behind why a teacher might choose to use a certain teaching approach. The take-home handout How Students Learn Best focuses on a summary of current research findings and provides them, as parents, with a way to be discerning about the teaching approaches used at their school.

The second part of today's session will focus on different **learning styles** and how helping our children know more about their own learning styles can help them be more effective learners.

Experiencing Different Teaching Approaches (25 minutes)

1. Briefly introduce the activity. Tell participants that in the next 15 minutes or so, they will participate in a very abbreviated series of activities, each of which **exemplifies a different teaching approach**. The purpose is to provide them with some brief, common experiences to both illustrate and enliven the discussion about these different teaching approaches. The activities will be presented in a fraction of the time that students would ideally have, and are not meant to provide them with any more than a taste of the full experience.

2. Introduce the structured activity. Tell the participants that they will begin by doing a **structured activity.**

Explain that you have some powder for them to investigate. The powder is safe to handle, but they should please try to keep their work on the plates to control the mess. Add that the powder can be slightly irritating if it gets in your eyes (like soap), so they should wash their hands after handling it.

Show overhead transparency #2. (Don't take the time to read it aloud to the group.)

Participants will feel rushed. Do your best to keep the pace moving, even so. The goal is for them to briefly experience four different teaching approaches; the goal is not for them to finish each activity. In previous versions of this session, we gave participants more time to complete each challenge, and the universal reaction was that it was not a good use of their time. They preferred more time to reflect on the experience as adults.

Structured Activity

1. Add 10 drops of water to each of the piles of powder and record your observations (what you see).

2. Predict what will happen when you add 3 more *spoonfuls* (1/2 teaspoons) of water to each pile. Go ahead and do it.

3. What changes did you notice—now that the powder has *absorbed* all the water?

Tell them they will have about 5 minutes to follow the three steps of this structured activity. If they were students, you would give them much longer. Since they won't have much time, you would like them to follow the steps and pay attention to their experience of doing a structured activity. Tell them that you will give them a time signal for when they need to move on.

3. Participants conduct the structured activity. Distribute the materials. Circulate around the room as needed to encourage everyone to participate. After several minutes give them a 2-minute warning.

4. Conclude the structured activity. Tell them that if this were a class of students, you would take the time to ask them a few questions about what they observed. You're going to skip that today, and instead immediately ask them, "What did you wonder about this powder?" Record several of their responses on a blank overhead entitled, "Questions We Have." Conclude by saying that this was a structured activity.

5. Introduce the open-ended exploration. Tell the participants that they will continue to investigate this mystery substance, but this time through an **open-ended exploration.**

Show overhead transparency #3. (Don't read it aloud to the group.)

Open-ended Exploration

Find out as much as you can about what will happen when you add two different solutions to the mystery substance.

Say, you will give them two different solutions: sugar water and salt water. Their job is to find out as much as they can about what will happen when they add two different solutions to the substance on their plates. (Note: they will be adding the solutions to the piles of PSA to which they have already added water. There is no need to start with fresh piles of PSA.)

Point out that they have their four piles of substance to work with, and they can decide as a group how to investigate those piles. Tell them to try to come up with a plan first and make a prediction about what will happen, before testing out their ideas. They can proceed however they like, as long as the group agrees on the procedure. Mention that because they have just five minutes to finish this part of the activity, they should not spend too long in planning!

6. Participants conduct the open-ended exploration. Distribute the cups of the two solutions—sugar water and salt water. Circulate around the room making sure they understand what they are to do. Groups of adults (unlike groups of children!) sometimes have difficulty engaging in an unstructured investigation. Encourage groups to feel comfortable in trying anything they'd like. Emphasize that there is no right or wrong approach. After several minutes give them a 2-minute warning.

7. Conclude the open-ended exploration. Have the groups put all the materials back on the tray and take the tray to an area that you designate. (Even adults won't be able to resist tinkering with the materials if they are left in front of them!)

Hold a brief discussion about their investigations. What happened when the solutions were added? Did both liquids react in the same way with the substance on the plate? What did they discover? Conclude by saying this was the open-ended exploration.

Note: the purpose of revisiting the question list after each activity is for participants to notice how a particular teaching approach caused them to wonder or not. If repeatedly revisiting "Questions We Have" becomes awkward or bogs down the flow, then you might want to skip it. Use your discretion.

Again, ask if they have any new questions about the substance. Record their questions on the "Questions We Have" overhead that was started earlier in the session.

8. Introduce the read and answer activity. Show overhead transparency #4. (Don't read it aloud to the group.)

Read and Answer Activity

Read the information sheet and answer the questions.

Tell the participants that they will now do a **read and answer activity.** Tell them that they will have about five minutes to read an information sheet and answer the questions.

9. Participants conduct the read and answer activity. Distribute the Information about PSA and Questions to Answer on PSA sheets. After several minutes give them a 2-minute warning. If participants seem concerned by the time limit, go ahead and reassure them that it's okay if they don't finish!

10. Conclude the read and answer activity. After about five minutes, get the group's attention again. Point out that read and answer is a teaching approach that many of us are quite familiar with. Ask them if the reading helped to answer any of the questions that came up during the first two activities. Did it leave them with new questions?

11. Introduce the problem-solving challenge. Explain to the group that as a team, they will now conduct a **problem-solving challenge.** Show overhead transparency #5. (Don't read it aloud to the group.)

Problem-solving Challenge

Think up a practical use for the powder in a real-world situation. Make sure to take into account what you now know about the properties of the powder.

Draw a picture of how the product would be used and write an advertising slogan so people will see how useful it will be.

Tell them that their challenge is to come up with a practical use for the powder in a real-world situation (that could make them all millionaires!). With just five minutes to begin this challenge they probably won't have enough time to do more than think of a use and talk about it in their group. But if they did have time, they could jot down a few ideas or advertising slogans, or even draw a picture of their idea showing how they have applied what they learned about the substance.

12. Participants conduct the problem-solving challenge. Circulate among the groups, making sure they understand what they are to do. After several minutes give them a 2-minute warning. Again, reassure them that it's okay if they don't finish!

13. Conclude the problem-solving challenge. After about five minutes, get the group's attention again. Ask several groups to share their idea of how the PSA powder could be used. Conclude by reminding them that this was a problem-solving challenge.

Among the uses for super absorbents are: as fuel filters, to keep water out of the gas tank; in rootballs, dipped in a super absorbent, to hold moisture while replanting; as seed coating to help in germination; in bandages, to help keep wounds dry; in baby diapers, baby powder, and sanitary napkins to absorb bodily fluids; and in ice packs with a super absorbent that also retains heat and cold.

Recently, an enterprising fire fighter (after noticing that water-soaked disposable diapers often do not burn in house fires) discovered that PSA has fire retardant properties. He has used PSA mixed with water to create a fire retardant spray which can be applied to the outside of houses.

Debrief of Learning Activities (20 minutes)

1. Pass out the debrief cards. Ask the participants to become adults again as they reflect on the experience of each of the teaching approaches. They will have about five minutes to talk in their small groups. Emphasize that they should try collectively to answer the questions on the card.

Show overhead #6. Say that you have summarized the four teaching approaches that they experienced on the overhead.

Overview of Teaching Approaches

Structured Activity
(Follow the directions. Add water to powder.
Predict what will happen when you add more water.)

Open-ended Exploration
(Explore what happens when two solutions are added.)

Read and Answer Activity
(Read about PSA and answer questions.)

Problem-solving Challenge
(Design a practical use for PSA powder.)

2. Have small groups discuss questions on cards.
What were your impressions of each learning activity?
Which one did you like the best?
Which one did you learn the most from?
Which one encouraged you to ask questions?
Which made you want to do more experiments?

3. Discuss the activities. After about five minutes, get the attention of the entire group. Show overhead #7.

Which Teaching Approaches are Best for

1) Generating high interest and curiosity?

2) Helping to understand information and concepts?

3) Encouraging thinking and questions?

Ask, "What generalizations do you think can be made about each teaching approach?"

Facilitate the discussion to give participants a chance to discuss the strengths and weaknesses of each approach. Ask, for example:

- What did you see as the strengths of the open-ended exploration? The structured activity? The read and answer activity? The problem-solving challenge?

- Were you surprised by any of your reactions?

- Did you feel more comfortable with one approach than another?

4. Discuss some possible goals connected to different approaches.

Point out that as they discovered, it's not a matter of good and bad teaching approaches. There are different approaches with different strengths. The choices for different approaches can sometimes depend on the goals of the lesson. Show overhead transparency #8.

Consider the Goals of the Lesson

Open-ended Exploration
—introduce new area
—generate curiosity and interest
—foster positive attitudes about science

Structured Activity
—encourage specific questions
—model one way of investigating
—lead to deeper investigations

Problem-solving Challenge
—apply new-found knowledge
—provide a sense of accomplishment

Read and Answer Activity
—provide information

Depending on the content of the group discussion you just had, you may want to add a few points from the overhead transparency. Or you may want to just let the overhead stand to summarize what was already said in the discussion.

5. Continue by making the following key points:

- Different teaching approaches accomplish different things.

- Research tells us that all of these different teaching approaches are necessary for best learning (and that all students need to experience a balance of each).

- There are better (and worse) ways to sequence individual learning experiences. (Specifically, that learning happens most naturally when students begin with open-ended exploration type activities before they get information through reading/lecture.)

6. Emphasize that there is no set formula. In spite of what we do know about learning, point out that there is not a rigid prescription about how to construct learning experiences for children and no one set formula about the best mix of different approaches for all situations.

Point out that various combinations of approaches can build student learning in a constructive way, maintain student and teacher interest, add variety, and reach students with different learning styles and strengths. Each teacher is faced with the challenge of constructing a curriculum for her classroom; there is a fair amount of artistry involved.

Show overhead transparency #9.

**Reasons Why a Teacher Might Choose a
Particular Approach or Sequence of Approaches**

· the subject matter
· the instructional materials used
· the experience and age of students
· the requirements of the district, state, or nation
· the experience, training, and preference of the teacher
· the time available

Explain that in addition to the goals of the lesson, there are
many reasons why a teacher might choose a particular approach or sequence of approaches. There is no one set formula!

7. Two examples. While each of these points could warrant a
long discussion, you might want to give two examples to indicate the complexity of the situation:

• Teachers don't choose, but are expected to use, a school
district's adopted curriculum. So, for instance, in the case
where there is a weak mathematics curriculum, it may take a
teacher a year or two to get to know the curriculum and to
know how to supplement its deficiencies or adapt it for the
diverse learners in her classroom.

• Just as different learners have different comfort levels with
each approach, different teachers have different comfort levels with each approach. So, for instance, in the case where a
district has adopted a state-of-the-art inquiry-based science
curriculum, a teacher unfamiliar with these approaches
might have a very hard time being able to deliver that curriculum. So she modifies the adopted curriculum.

These two examples represent good and not-so-good reasons
why teachers choose to supplement or substitute for existing
materials.

**8. It's not easy to meet the needs of all students and all fami-
lies.** Having a diverse group of students makes decisions
about what learning experiences to provide to students difficult. Parents expectations for what should happen in the classroom are usually divergent, too. In these times of growing diversity, it is difficult to know how to face the challenge of providing an educational system that will meet the needs of all
students and all families. It isn't easy to reach a consensus of
what the mix of approaches should be.

What Research Says About Learning
(5 minutes)

1. Five research findings. Say that you *will* leave them with some absolutes about what is strongly supported by research. Show transparency #10.

How Students Learn Best

- Active learning is best.
- Understanding goes beyond vocabulary.
- There are recognized phases of learning.
- Students of different ages have different needs.
- A balanced diet of learning is the healthiest!

Tell them that you have a handout giving more details about each one of these points that they can take home with them. Point out that in the handout, each point concludes with what effective teachers do to address this point. Knowing what research says about learning, and how this looks in what a teacher does, prepares us as parents to be more discerning about what we see happening in our children's classrooms. Another handout focuses on "the art of the question" and how best to respond to children's questions to encourage their active learning.

Say just a few words about each of these five points.

- **Active learning is best.** While reading and listening play a role, there is overwhelming evidence that lasting learning and retention of information require that students interact with materials and ideas.

Effective teachers involve students in learning by doing, working in groups, discussing, writing, and reflecting, *in addition to* reading and listening.

- **Understanding goes beyond vocabulary.** Facts and formulas are important in math and science. However, true understanding involves a much deeper approach to learning about concepts. Learning concepts takes longer than rote memorization. Students need to interact with ideas.

Effective teachers seek to present topics in greater depth in order to deepen student understanding.

- **There are recognized phases of learning.** Students need chances to explore phenomena and ideas, receive information, and apply what they have learned to new situations. They need to investigate their own questions. Different teaching approaches are better for each goal.

Effective teachers know how to sequence these types of activities so that students learn best.

- **Students of different ages have different needs.** Younger students need lots of free exploration and experiential learning. Older students are capable of more abstract thinking and of applying what they have learned to more complex situations. Research shows that *all learners* need direct interaction with materials.

Effective teachers know how to provide students of different ages/developmental levels with the experiences they need.

- **A balanced diet of learning is the healthiest!** A diverse menu of learning experiences is best. ALL learners need to experience all approaches to learning.

An effective teacher provides a balance of different learning approaches.

2. Take the long view. As parents we should try to have a long-range perspective. Realize your child's education is made up of all their life experiences. Parents can help provide the balance by offering a wide diversity of experiences. Strive to achieve balance over many grades, at home as well as at school.

Multiple Intelligences and Different Learning Styles (15 minutes)

1. Introduce the idea of learning styles. Tell the participants that when designing learning experiences for the classroom, a teacher also needs to take into account the fact that students have different learning styles. Some people, for example, tend to be more "visual learners." Others take in information better through their ears—they could be called "auditory learners." Still others learn best by touching and through physical movement, and others learn best by reading about something. It is very helpful for parents to be aware of the ways their children learn best, and help children come to know their strengths and how they learn best. Parents can also help children develop their abilities to learn in other ways as well. A good teacher does the same. All of us reflect different combinations of these ways of learning.

2. Participants complete inventory. Explain that in order to learn a little more about their own learning styles, you would like participants to take their own "multiple intelligences inventory." Emphasize that this is not meant to be a test and there are no right or wrong answers. It is just a few questions to give them a sense of some of their strengths. Hopefully, it will be interesting to them. Also make clear that the number of checks does not indicate anyone's level of intelligence or ability in that category—just that they may have strength or interest in that particular area. By reflecting on their own capabilities, they can begin to recognize how these different strengths may be reflected in their children. Pass out the Multiple Intelligences Inventory for Adults sheets and tell them that they have about five minutes to complete the inventory checklist.

3. Explain multiple intelligences. In recent years, many educators have taken this idea of different learning styles to a new level. In their sincere efforts to reach all students, these educators have found the ideas of Howard Gardner, a Harvard professor, to be extremely useful. Gardner originated the theory of "multiple intelligences." He was seeking a way to describe and define the many capabilities that help people solve problems and achieve success in all the different fields of human endeavor. He questioned the idea that you could determine intelligence, as on an IQ test, by taking a person out of their natural learning environment and asking them to do isolated tasks they had never done before and might never do again. Instead he proposed that all human beings have at least seven intelligences, seven sets of abilities, that help them solve problems and create things in the real world. As he puts it, "it's not how smart you are, but *how* you are smart!"

4. Show overhead summarizing multiple intelligences. Show overhead transparency #11. Don't read the whole page aloud.

Multiple Intelligences

1) **Linguistic:** The capacity to use words effectively, orally or in writing.

2) **Logical-Mathematical:** The ability to use numbers effectively and reason well.

3) **Spatial:** The ability to perceive the visual and spatial world accurately, including the ability to visualize and sensitivity to color, line, shape, form, and space.

4) **Bodily-Kinesthetic:** The ability to use one's whole body to express ideas and feelings, and to fashion or transform with one's hands.

5) **Musical:** The ability to sense, distinguish between, and express oneself in musical forms, including sensitivity to rhythm, pitch, melody, and tone color.

6) **Interpersonal:** The capacity to perceive and distinguish differences in the motivations and feelings of others and to work well with others.

7) **Intrapersonal:** The capacity for self-knowledge and understanding, and the ability to act based on that knowledge.

Read the main headings aloud. Allow participants to read silently if they want, but mainly let them know that they will get this information on a handout that they can take home with them. **Emphasize that all of us possess all seven intelligences, in different degrees and combinations.** Add that they are not listed in order of importance. You may want to mention that other intelligences have also been proposed—the exact number is not important, just the idea that there are "multiple intelligences" is what is most important.

5. Share responses within small groups. Ask participants to hold brief discussions within their table groups about their reactions to the multiple intelligences inventory. Tell them that, in each group, each person should have the opportunity to share at least one feeling, comment, or idea that came up as they were completing the inventory. The group may also want to discuss any thoughts the inventory raised about their children's capabilities and multiple intelligences. Circulate among the groups as they discuss.

6. "Blended" intelligences. Gain the attention of the whole group one more time. Say that you were able to hear snippets of fascinating discussion at each group. If appropriate, add a bit more about how we each use our various intelligences in a "blended way." People use a repertoire of these different types of intelligences, to varying degrees and in different combinations, in order to solve the problems we face in everyday life and to express our own individual talents. Most people develop competency in many areas and it is true that there are lots of different ways to demonstrate intelligence in each category. Usually the "intelligences" work together in very complex ways to produce the special skills and abilities we see in every individual. For example, a violinist in an orchestra, in addition to musical intelligence and the ability to read music, must have a high degree of bodily-kinesthetic intelligence and strong interpersonal skills as well.

7. How to help your child know his/her strengths/challenges. Tell participants that there are several handouts on multiple intelligences to take with them when they leave the workshop—one which provides a bit more information on the theory itself and the other which may help them think about their children's capabilities from this perspective. Emphasize that, with their child of elementary school age, they may want to point out that they are "smart" in all of these ways, but may be "smarter" or have a more innate ability in some of them. It may also be helpful to say that even though some abilities may come easier to a child than others, when a more challenging area is worked on, it can become one of his or her greatest strengths! It is important to point out to children that hard work and practice can help all of us excel in all areas.

Conclusion (5 minutes)

1. Tie the two parts of the session together. Point out that the first part of the session focused on teaching approaches; the second part on learning styles. Explain that people often confuse the two. It is important for *all* students to experience many different teaching approaches (regardless of their particular learning styles). All people have different learning styles—knowing their learning strengths and challenges can help know how to approach different learning situations.

2. Distribute take-home sheets. Set the take-home handouts and the Research Reference list on a table so parents can take what they'd like when they leave.

3. If you're planning to present other sessions, let them know when and where and encourage them to bring other parents.

4. Be sure to thank all the participants for coming and for the ideas and comments they've shared. If you have a feedback or evaluation form for the participants, urge them to complete it so presentations can be improved in the future.

Going Further

Participants could benefit from having time to discuss and practice applying some of the ideas presented in this session. This could be done by providing several scenarios and asking small groups of participants to discuss what they could do in each situation. Scenarios could include the following:

> a. Your child comes home from school saying that science is boring and that all they do is read. What could you do?
>
> b. The mathematics curriculum in your child's class is rich in problem solving experiences but you are concerned that your child is not mastering her math facts. What could you do?
>
> c. You notice that your child's 2nd grade teacher isn't teaching science. When you ask, she says that there's no time in the day because the needs of focusing on reading and writing are so great. What could you do?
>
> d. Your child is strong in mathematics. The program at school seems to be fine but you sense that she needs more. What could you do?
>
> e. Your 5th grader's "logical-mathematical" intelligence is not his strength but he has exceptional "linguistic" intelligence. He has a hard time with mathematics. What could you do?

Information about PSA

So what exactly *is* the mystery powder?

The powder used in our investigations is actually a synthetic (human-made) chemical, called poly sodium acrylate, or "PSA" for short. It is also sometimes called a "super slurper." It is made by combining sodium acrylate and acrylic acid to produce a large molecule called a polymer. Polymers are long, winding, chains made up of thousands of smaller molecules linked together. The amazing thing about this particular polymer is that it can absorb as much as eight hundred times its own weight in water. This is because of its unique structure. It is a large, twisted, molecule resembling a tree with tangled branches. These branches have highly charged carboxyl groups hanging from them which attract the water molecules. As water is added to the "super slurper," the "tree" swells up into a gel-like substance which does not dissolve easily and continues to grow with each water molecule that is absorbed onto its "branches."

What are polymers?

Polymers are long, winding chains made up of thousands of smaller molecules linked together. (*Poly* means many; *mer* means part.) Natural polymers are made by plants and animals including, those in hair, the cellulose in plants, the wool in sheep, and fibers made by insects. Starch is a natural polymer made from glucose—a polysaccharide made up of long chains of glucose. Polymers can also be made synthetically from chemicals. All plastics and many of the clothes we wear are made in his way. Many fibers used in clothing, carpets and fabrics are made from polymers. Wool, cotton, and silk come from plants and animals. Synthetic fibers such as nylon, acrylic, and polyester come from oil. Synthetic fibers are less costly and stronger than many natural materials. Polymers can be designed for specific purposes.

How does the salt water change the gel?

The salt water dissolves the gel by taking away its ability to attract water molecules. Salt water contains charged ions which neutralize the carboxyl groups on the PSA molecule. When the salt is added, the PSA "lets go" of the water and the gel becomes liquefied.

Where did super-absorbent chemicals come from?

Super-absorbents were originally developed by the U.S. Department of Agriculture. During the oil crisis of the 1970s, scientists began to study ways starch could be used to replace petroleum in many consumer items. Experiments were conducted using synthetic chemicals, attaching them to a long starch molecule. One of the first of these products was a starch and polyacrylonitrile co-polymer which they named "Super Slurper." This new material had unique properties unlike the separate properties of either the starch or the added chemical. As described by co-inventor Mary Olliden Weaver, this molecule could absorb hundreds of times its weight in water. Since then, many new types of polymers have been made from starch—some of these can hold up to 5,000 times their weight in water!

Questions to Answer
on PSA

Explain in your own words how PSA holds in the water.

What is a polymer?

Name three polymers that exist in nature.

How does salt cause PSA to "let go" of the water?

Multiple Intelligences Inventory for Adults

Check the statements that apply in each category.

Linguistic Intelligence

____ Books are very important to me.

____ I enjoy word games like Scrabble, Anagrams, or Password.

____ I enjoy writing.

____ I appreciate tongue twisters, nonsense rhymes, and puns.

____ I like to tell stories and jokes.

____ I am a good speller.

Logical-Mathematical Intelligence

____ I can quickly compute numbers in my head.

____ Math and/or science were enjoyable subjects in school.

____ I enjoy playing strategy games and solving logic puzzles and brainteasers.

____ I think on a more abstract or conceptual level than some people.

____ My mind searches for patterns, regularities, and logical sequences.

____ I believe that almost everything has a logical explanation.

Spatial Intelligence

____ I can see clear visual images when I imagine things.

____ I enjoy doing jigsaw puzzles, mazes, and other visual puzzles.

____ I can generally find my way around unfamiliar territory.

____ I like to draw or doodle.

____ Geometry was easier for me than algebra in school.

____ I prefer reading text that is illustrated with maps, charts, and diagrams.

Bodily-Kinesthetic Intelligence

____ I engage in at least one physical activity or sport on a regular basis.

____ I frequently use hand gestures or other forms of body language when conversing with someone.

____ I like to touch things in order to learn about them.

____ My best ideas come to me when I'm out for a long walk or engaging in some other physical activity.

____ I like working with my hands (sewing, needlepoint, carving, carpentry, model building).

____ I prefer practicing a new skill rather than reading about it or seeing a video describing the activity.

Multiple Intelligences Inventory for Adults

Musical Intelligence

___ I can tell when a musical note is off key.

___ I have a pleasant singing voice.

___ I often make tapping sounds or hum little melodies.

___ I play a musical instrument.

___ I remember melodies of songs.

___ I respond favorably to music.

Interpersonal Intelligence

___ I have at least three close friends.

___ When I have a problem, I'm more likely to seek out another
person to talk to about it than to work it out on my own.

___ I enjoy socializing.

___ I'm the sort of person people come to for advice.

___ I enjoy the challenge of teaching another person (or groups of people)
what I know how to do.

___ I have natural leadership qualities.

Intrapersonal Intelligence

___ I regularly spend time alone meditating, reflecting, or thinking about
important life questions.

___ I have a special hobby or interest that I keep pretty much to myself.

___ I have a realistic view of my strengths and weaknesses.

___ I am aware of my feelings.

___ I am fairly self-directed.

___ I am confident and comfortable being different from others in a group.

Adapted from: *7 Kinds of Smart: Discovering and Using Your Natural Intelligence*,
Thomas Armstrong, Plume/Penguin, New York, 1993.

Debrief Card

What were your impressions of each learning activity?

Which one did you like the best?

Which one did you learn the most from?

Which one encouraged you to ask questions?

Which made you want to do more experiments?

- ✂

Debrief Card

What were your impressions of each learning activity?

Which one did you like the best?

Which one did you learn the most from?

Which one encouraged you to ask questions?

Which made you want to do more experiments?

Goals for the Session

- Consider different teaching approaches and their strengths in helping students learn

- Receive a summary of what research says about how students learn best

- Discuss the theory of "multiple intelligences" and current thinking about different learning styles

- Take home suggestions for you to help your child know more about his/her own learning style to become a more effective learner

Structured Activity

1. Add 10 drops of water to each of the piles of powder and record your observations (what you see).

2. Predict what will happen when you add 3 more *spoonfuls* (1/2 teaspoons) of water to each pile. Go ahead and do it.

3. What changes did you notice—now that the powder has *absorbed* all the water?

Open-ended Exploration

Find out as much as you can about what will happen when you add two different solutions to the mystery substance.

Read and Answer Activity

Read the information sheet and answer the questions.

Problem-solving Challenge

Think up a practical use for the powder in a real-world situation. Make sure to take into account what you now know about the properties of the powder.

Draw a picture of how the product would be used and write an advertising slogan so people will see how useful it will be.

Overview of Teaching Approaches

Structured Activity
(Follow the directions. Add water to powder.
Predict what will happen when you add more
water.)

Open-ended Exploration
(Explore what happens when two solutions
are added.)

Read and Answer Activity
(Read about PSA and answer questions.)

Problem-solving Challenge
(Design a practical use for PSA powder.)

Which Teaching Approaches are Best for

1) Generating high interest and curiosity?

2) Helping to understand information and concepts?

3) Encouraging thinking and questions?

Consider the Goals
of the Lesson

Open-ended Exploration
—introduce new area
—generate curiosity and interest
—foster positive attitudes about science

Structured Activity
—encourage specific questions
—model one way of investigating
—lead to deeper investigations

Problem-solving Challenge
—apply new-found knowledge
—provide a sense of accomplishment

Read and Answer Activity
—provide information

Reasons Why a Teacher Might Choose a Particular Approach or Sequence of Approaches

- the subject matter

- the instructional materials used

- the experience and age of students

- the requirements of the district, state, or nation

- the experience, training, and preference of the teacher

- the time available

How Students Learn Best

- Active learning is best.

- Understanding goes beyond vocabulary.

- There are recognized phases of learning.

- Students of different ages have different needs.

- A balanced diet is healthiest!

Multiple Intelligences

1) **Linguistic:** The capacity to use words effectively, orally or in writing.

2) **Logical-Mathematical:** The ability to use numbers effectively and reason well.

3) **Spatial:** The ability to perceive the visual and spatial world accurately, including the ability to visualize and sensitivity to color, line, shape, form, and space.

4) **Bodily-Kinesthetic:** The ability to use one's whole body to express ideas and feelings, and to fashion or transform with one's hands.

5) **Musical:** The ability to sense, distinguish between, and express oneself in musical forms, including sensitivity to rhythm, pitch, melody, and tone color.

6) **Interpersonal:** The capacity to perceive and distinguish differences in the motivations and feelings of others and to work well with others.

7) **Intrapersonal:** The capacity for self-knowledge and understanding, and the ability to act based on that knowledge.

Learning Memories

I don't remember studying science at all in elementary school. All I recall of science in middle and high school was trying to remember stuff I never understood. At the time, the science teacher I considered best, Ms. T., was one that gave us ways to memorize—you know, things like ROY-G-BIV to remember the order of the colors in the rainbow. It's true that I will always remember red-orange-yellow-green-blue-indigo-violet, but to this day I don't know the significance of it!

I enjoyed math in elementary school, in spite of my heart-pounding and utter panic during "speed tests." I was a product of the first "new math" and for me, it worked. I liked learning about properties of operations and learning why things worked. It was very empowering. Life changed when I got to fifth grade and multiplication of fractions. I remember crying at home with my mother, telling her that I didn't understand why when you multiply two things together it resulted in an answer that was smaller. My mom called my teacher, Ms. M., and asked if she could spend some extra time with me. I'll never forget Ms. M. telling me not to worry that I didn't understand, because I knew how get the right answers anyway. It was that year that I gave up trying to understand.

I remember my 9th grade math teacher Mr. C. He was in his first year of teaching and therefore rather edgy. He was a very tall man with a very large nose, and he wore the ugliest ties imaginable. Being normal teenagers, we all used to laugh at him behind his back. Mr. C. had the aura of being mean. A lot of kids were terrified of him and of math. He used to stand on the desk and yell out formulas. He was also known to stand on the desk and throw down the textbook with brute force in order to get our attention. But, nevertheless, he loved math, and to me personally, that was strongly communicated. Since I too loved math, he was quite nice to me. He gave praise all the time and was very encouraging to me and other students who showed any interest in the subject. I also remember that in the class, the best 3 or 4 students were girls—and Mr. C. did not make any big deal or reference to this at all.

I have very positive memories of my 8th grade biology class. The teacher was very humorous and entertaining, but he also imparted a great deal of enthusiasm for everything we studied. He was fascinated by animals and their behavior—including humans! He was very hands-on, wanted us to do experiments and pursue every question with curiosity and a skeptical scientific view. He loved to challenge us and stretch our growing minds. His love for the subject and his enthusiasm were catching—even the most reluctant students found themselves learning and enjoying it. Later I found out that this teacher became the principal of the best high school in the city. He certainly had the people skills for that job, but I always felt bad for students who came after me because they were not able to experience his wonderful classroom teaching style.

How Students Learn Best

There is a large body of research evidence showing that no matter what a student's individual style or learning stage:

- **Active learning is best.** While reading and listening play a role in learning, there is overwhelming evidence that lasting learning and retention of information require that students interact with materials and ideas. An effective teacher is one that involves students in learning by doing, working in groups, discussing, writing, and reflecting—in addition to reading and listening.

- **Understanding goes beyond vocabulary.** Facts and formulas are important in math and science. However, true understanding involves a much deeper approach to learning about concepts. Learning concepts takes longer than rote memorization. Effective teachers seek to present topics in greater depth in order to deepen student understanding.

- **There are recognized phases of learning.** Students need chances to explore phenomena and ideas, receive information, apply what they have learned to new situations, and investigate their own questions. Effective teachers know how to sequence these types of activities so that students learn best.

- **Students of different ages have different needs.** Younger students need lots of free exploration and experiential learning opportunities. Older students are more capable of abstract thinking and of applying what they have learned to more complex situations. Research shows that they still need direct interaction with materials. Effective teachers know how to provide students of different ages with the experiences they need.

- **A balanced diet is healthiest!** There's a diverse menu of learning experiences available—hands-on experiments, reading an article, listening to a parent talk about science in his or her career, making a model of the solar system, writing a letter to Bill Gates about a new invention, watching a video, acting out a chemical process, working together on group presentations—these are just a few examples. It is good for all children to experience all approaches to learning. Most educators, like nutritionists, recommend a balanced diet. An effective teacher provides a balance of different learning approaches.

Sample Questions to Encourage Learning

Questions to use with your child to encourage thinking and learning in any situation (nature walks, museum visits, homework lessons…)

What did you observe?

What do you think happened?

What happened when…?

What do we know now?

What did you discover about…?

What do you mean by…?

Can you explain why? Do you have an explanation for…?

What might another explanation be?

Can you compare this with something else?

How is this the same or different from..?

What other factors might be involved?

What did you find out?

What questions do you have?

What could we do to find out?

How could we test our ideas?

How can you use what you just found out to solve this
    particular problem?

How do you know that your solution is correct?

How did you arrive at the solution?

Why do you think that?

Tell me more about your idea.

THE ART OF THE QUESTION

Effective teachers know that learning to ask good questions is a crucial part of teaching. Parents can also use questions to promote thinking. Open-ended questions ("Why do you think the butterfly flew away?") are more likely to encourage creative thinking than close-ended ones ("How many antennae does a butterfly have?"). Some questions provoke more complex thinking; others ask for information. Both kinds of questions have their place.

When a child asks you a question, one good first strategy is to turn it around and say, "That's a good question. What do you think?" Asking for your child's ideas about finding out more is also a good strategy. Teachers know that answers to questions, whether correct or incorrect, can be very revealing. By listening to their answers and asking children to explain their thinking, you can see their level of understanding.

Suppose your child gives a wrong answer? Avoid a negative or judgmental response—a "wrong" answer can be a great opportunity for learning. Asking, "What made you think that?" or "How did you arrive at that answer?" can reveal the thinking behind the answer and often allows a child to figure out a new approach on their own. Treat some "correct" answers with the same scrutiny as incorrect ones, so your child will not be tipped off when you ask, "What made you think that?" All answers can be questioned—even those that sound "correct" at first—science is all about questioning! It's important for teachers and parents to openly acknowledge when they don't know the answer to a question, and to model ways to find it out—ask someone who might know, look in a book, consult the Internet, ask a librarian, conduct an experiment, or, together, analyze the problem again.

WHAT ARE "MULTIPLE INTELLIGENCES?"

Harvard psychology professor Howard Gardner first presented his theory of "multiple intelligences" in his 1983 book, *Frames of Mind*. Since then, his ideas have been widely discussed and been of great interest to educators. His theory proposes that all human beings possess *at least* seven intelligences. It attempts to take into account the findings of modern brain science and psychology. Gardner sees "intelligence" as a biological and psychological **potential** that is capable of being realized to a greater or lesser extent, depending on one's experience, education, social environment, and other factors. The seven intelligences described by Gardner, briefly summarized, are:

• **Linguistic Intelligence:** The capacity to use words effectively, whether orally or in writing. This includes the ability to manipulate the structure and syntax of language, the sounds of language, the meanings of language, and the practical uses of language, such as for explaining, remembering, persuading, etc.

• **Logical-Mathematical Intelligence:** The capacity to use numbers effectively and to reason well. This includes awareness of logical patterns and relationships, functions, and cause and effect.

• **Spatial Intelligence:** The ability to perceive the visual and spatial world accurately, including sensitivity to color, line, shape, form, space, and the relationships between them. Includes the capacity to visualize, make graphic representations, and orient oneself in spatial surroundings.

• **Bodily-Kinesthetic Intelligence:** The ability to use one's whole body to express ideas and feelings, and the ability to fashion or transform with one's hands. Includes skills such as coordination, balance, dexterity, strength, flexibility, speed, and other physical skills.

• **Musical Intelligence:** The ability to perceive, distinguish between, and express oneself in musical forms. Includes sensitivities to rhythm, pitch or melody, timbre and tone color. Can apply to either an intuitive grasp of music, an analytic or technical understanding of it, or both.

• **Interpersonal Intelligence:** The capacity to perceive and distinguish differences in the moods, intentions, motivations, and feelings of others. Includes sensitivity to facial expressions, gestures, and body language. This intelligence also includes the ability to respond to these cues effectively, to work well with others, and to lead.

• **Intrapersonal Intelligence:** The capacity for self-knowledge and understanding, and the ability to act on the basis of that knowledge. Includes having an accurate picture of one's own strengths and limitations, inner moods, intentions, feelings, motivations, needs, desires, and a capacity for self-discipline and self-esteem.

The theory of multiple intelligences emphasizes that all of us possess all seven intelligences, and each of us possesses them in different degrees and combinations. As Gardner says, "It is of the utmost importance that we recognize and nurture all of the varied human intelligences, and all of the combinations of intelligences. We are all so different largely because we all have different combinations of intelligences. If we recognize this, I think we will have at least a better chance of dealing appropriately with the many problems that we face in the world." Gardner and others emphasize that the exact number of "intelligences" is less important than the idea that there are many kinds. He has discussed a "Naturalist Intelligence," saying, "...the individual who is able readily to recognize flora and fauna, to make other...distinctions in the natural world, and to use this ability productively...is exercising an important intelligence and one that is not adequately encompassed on the current list." He has also referred to a "Spiritual Intelligence." The ability to blend or synthesize different intelligences so they work well together has been called a "Synthetic Intelligence." Whether seven, eight, or more "intelligences" are described, the most revolutionary idea in Gardner's work is that there *are* multiple intelligences. Viewed in this way, human intelligence is not restricted to only the more narrow linguistic and mathematical abilities measured by most standardized tests and traditionally described in school as being "smart." As Gardner has been quoted as saying, "It's not how smart you are, but *how* you are smart!"

These ideas have had a significant impact on education. A number of schools around the country are seeking to put them into practice. More and more teachers, when assessing student achievement, are finding ways for students to work within their areas of strength to demonstrate what they have learned, as well as finding ways to encourage students to further develop other abilities and "intelligences" that may be more challenging for them. Gardner's work speaks directly to teachers adapting a variety of learning formats for students with differing learning styles, and to the belief that education works most effectively if the unique blend of ways that people learn, think, and feel is taken into account.

If you're interested in learning more about multiple intelligences, here are some recommended books.

Frames of Mind: The Theory of Multiple Intelligences, Howard Gardner, HarperCollins Publishers, New York, 1983.

The Unschooled Mind: How Children Think and How Schools Should Teach, Howard Gardner, HarperCollins Publishers, New York, 1992.

Multiple Intelligences: The Theory in Practice, Howard Gardner, HarperCollins Publishers, New York, 1993.

In Their Own Way: Discovering and Encouraging Your Child's Personal Learning Style, Thomas Armstrong, Jeremy P. Tarcher Publishers, Los Angeles, 1987.

7 Kinds of Smart: Discovering and Using Your Natural Intelligence, Thomas Armstrong, Plume/Penguin, New York, 1993.

Multiple Intelligences in the Classroom, Thomas Armstrong, Association for Supervision and Curriculum Development, Alexandria, Virginia, 1994.

MULTIPLE INTELLIGENCES AND YOUR CHILDREN

Research supports the idea that children benefit from reflecting upon their own learning processes. Having a conversation with your child about their strengths can help them to chose appropriate ways to solve problems for themselves and can provide you with insights to help them develop to their fullest potential. Explain to your child that everybody is "smart" in different ways. Knowing your own **strengths** helps you know the easiest ways for you to learn. Explain that the questions are meant to get them thinking about the different ways they are smart and about how they learn most easily.

Here are some suggestions for questions to begin a discussion with your child about multiple intelligences:

Word Smart
Do you like to read books or listen to stories?
Do you like word games like Scrabble and Password?
Do you like to tell jokes and appreciate rhymes, puns, and tongue twisters?

Number Smart
Do you like math?
Do you wonder about how things work?
Do you enjoy strategy games, logic puzzles, and brain teasers?

Picture Smart
Do you enjoy doing art projects?
Are you good at doing mazes and jigsaw puzzles?
Can you imagine pictures in your mind?
Do you like to draw or doodle?

Body Smart
Do you like sports?
Do you like to learn by watching or by doing?
Do you like working with your hands? (building models, sewing, etc.)

Music Smart
Do you remember songs easily?
Do you like to play musical instruments, tap out rhythms, or sing?
Do you like to listen to music?

People Smart
Would you prefer to invite friends over (rather than playing by yourself)?
Do you have several different best friends?
Do you prefer talking about problems with someone or working them out yourself?

Self Smart
Do you like spending time alone?
Do you like thinking about what you want to do in the future?
Do you like to fit in with a group or are you happy to be a little different?

Adapted from: *7 Kinds of Smart: Discovering and Using Your Natural Intelligence*, Thomas Armstrong, Plume/Penguin, New York, 1993.

Assessing Your Children's Learning Habits

Consider the following learning habits as they relate to your children. Evaluate your children's strengths in each area by marking an "E" for excellent, "S" for satisfactory, or "N" for needs work. Then look for opportunities to build on strengths and work on weaknesses.

	Child 1	Child 2	Child 3
Motivation			
Child believes that her efforts make a difference and that she can succeed if she tries.	_____	_____	_____
Child believes it's worth trying even if it's hard, because it makes her feel successful.	_____	_____	_____
Child believes being smart is not just something she is born with, but something she can develop through her own efforts.	_____	_____	_____
Attention			
Child can stick with a project or task for a reasonable length of time.	_____	_____	_____
Child can persist if a task doesn't come easily.	_____	_____	_____
Child can shift attention when needed.	_____	_____	_____
Language			
Child can listen and remember what he hears.	_____	_____	_____
Child can express an idea with reasonable ease.	_____	_____	_____
Child can ask questions and get information.	_____	_____	_____
Child can take turns appropriately in conversations.	_____	_____	_____
Memory			
Child is aware that remembering things is important.	_____	_____	_____
Child uses memory "tricks" to remember certain things.	_____	_____	_____
Child knows that remembering takes effort.	_____	_____	_____

	CHILD 1	CHILD 2	CHILD 3
Problem Solving			
Child will try alternative ways to solve a problem.	_____	_____	_____
Child has confidence that she is a good problem solver.	_____	_____	_____
Child realizes that it's up to her to solve her own problems.	_____	_____	_____
Child knows that it feels good to solve a problem after "messing up" several times.	_____	_____	_____
Mindfulness			
Child takes the time to think about things.	_____	_____	_____
Child hears parents talk about the way they think about things.	_____	_____	_____
Child knows that he is responsible for the quality of his work.	_____	_____	_____
Child knows he must be able to talk about the ideas in what he is reading (rather than just sounding out words without much thought).	_____	_____	_____

Modified and adapted with permission from: *Helping Your Child Succeed in School: A Guide for Parents of 4 to 14 Year Olds*, by Popkin, Youngs, and Healy, Active Parenting Publishers, Atlanta, Georgia, 1995. Refer to this excellent resource for more in-depth information.

Session 2: Research References

Active Learning Is Best

*American Association for the Advancement of Science, Project 2061, *Benchmarks for Science Literacy*, Oxford University Press, New York, 1993, especially Chapter 15, "The Research Base."

Bredderman, T., "What Research Says: Activity Science—The Evidence Shows It Matters," *Science and Children*, 20(1), 39–41, 1982.

* Haury, D. L., Rillero, P., *Hands-On Approaches to Science Teaching: Questions and Answers from the Field and Research*, ERIC Clearinghouse, Columbus, Ohio, 1992.

* Kober, Nancy, *Ed Talk: What We Know About Science Teaching and Learning*, Council for Educational Development and Research, Washington, DC.

Kyle, W. C., Jr., et al., "What Research Says: Science Through Discovery: Students Love it," *Science and Children*, 23(2), 39–41, 1985, and "What Research Says About Hands-On Science," *Science and Children*, 25(2), 39–40, 1988.

* National Research Council/National Academy of Sciences, *National Science Education Standards*, National Academy Press, Washington, DC, 1996.

* Popkin, Michael H., Youngs, Bettie B., Healy, Jane M., *Helping Your Child Succeed in School: A Guide for Parents of 4 to 14 Year Olds*, Active Parenting Publishers, Atlanta, Georgia, 1995.

Shymansky, J. A., et al., "The Effects of New Science Curricula on Student Performance," *Journal of Research in Science Teaching*, 20, 387–404, 1983, and "A Reassessment of the Effects of Inquiry-Based Science Curricula of the 60's," *Journal of Research in Science Teaching*, 27(2), 127–144, 1990.

Understanding Goes Beyond Vocabulary

Glasson, G. E., "The Effects of Hands-on and Teacher Demonstration Laboratory Methods on Science Achievement in Relation to Reasoning Ability and Prior Knowledge," *Journal of Research in Science Teaching*, 26(2), 121–131, February, 1989.

* Haury, David L., *Teaching Science through Inquiry*, ERIC Clearinghouse for Science, Mathematics, and Environmental Education, March, 1993.

Lloyd, C. V., Contreras, N. J., "The Role of Experiences in Learning Science Vocabulary," Annual Meeting of the National Reading Conference, San Diego, ED 281 189

* Rakow, S. J., *Teaching Science as Inquiry*, Fastback 246. Phi Delta Kappa Educational Foundation, Bloomington, Indiana, 1986.

There are Recognized Phases of Learning

Baird, J., Fensham, P., Gunstone, R., White, R., "A Study of the Importance of Reflection for Improving Teaching and Learning," paper presented at National Association for Research in Science Teaching, San Francisco, 1989.

* Bredekamp, Sue, Copple, Carol, *Developmentally Appropriate Practice in Early Childhood Programs* (revised edition), National Association for the Education of Young Children, Washington, DC, 1997.

Carey, S., *Conceptual Change in Childhood*, MIT Press, Cambridge, Massachusetts, 1985.

Carey, S., Evans, R., Honda, M., Jay, E., Under, C., "An Experiment is When You Try It and See If It Works: A Study of Grade 7 Students' Understanding of the Construction of Scientific Knowledge," *International Journal of Science Education*, 11, 514–529, 1989.

* Driver, R., Guesne, E., Tiberghien, A., (eds) *Children's Ideas in Science,* Open University Press, Milton Keynes, UK, 1985.

Students of Different Ages have Different Needs

Grosslight, L., Unger, C., Jay, E., Smith, C.L., "Understanding Models and Their Use in Science: Conceptions of Middle and High School Students and Experts," *Journal of Research in Science Teaching*, 28, 799–822, 1991.

Leach, J., Driver, R., Scott, P., Wood-Robinson, C., *Progression in Understanding of Ecological Concepts by Pupils Aged 5–16*, Centre for Studies in Science and Mathematics Education, University of Leeds, UK, 1992.

* Lind, Karen K., *Exploring Science in Early Childhood: A Developmental Approach*, 2nd edition, Delmar Publishers, a division of International Thomson Publishing Inc., 1996.

* Shore, Rima, *Rethinking the Brain: New Insights into Early Development*, Families and Work Institute, New York, 1997.

Stavy, R., "Children's Ideas About Matter," *School Science and Mathematics*, 91, 240–244, 1991.

A Balanced Diet is Healthiest

Abruscato, J., *Teaching Children Science*, 3rd edition, Allyn & Bacon, Boston, 1992.

American Association for the Advancement of Science, Project 2061, *Benchmarks for Science Literacy*, Oxford University Press, New York, 1993.

Loucks-Horsley, S., et al., *Elementary School Science for the '90s*, The Network, Inc., Andover, Massachusetts, 1993.

National Research Council, *National Science Education Standards*, National Academy Press, Washington, DC, 1996.

* Rutherford, F.J., Ahlgren, A., *Science for All Americans*, Oxford University Press, New York, 1990.

Theory of Multiple Intelligences

* Armstrong, T., *7 Kinds of Smart: Discovering and Using Your Natural Intelligence*, Plume/Penguin, New York, 1993.

Armstrong, T., *In Their Own Way: Discovering and Encouraging Your Child's Personal Learning Style*, Jeremy P. Tarcher Publishers, Los Angeles, 1987.

Armstrong, T., *Multiple Intelligences in the Classroom*, Association for Supervision and Curriculum Development, Alexandria, Virginia, 1994.

* Gardner, H., *Frames of Mind: The Theory of Multiple Intelligences*, HarperCollins Publishers, New York, 1983.

* Gardner, H., *Multiple Intelligences: The Theory in Practice*, HarperCollins Publishers, New York, 1993.

Gardner, H., "Reflections on Multiple Intelligences: Myths and Messages," *Phi Delta Kappan*, November, 1995.

* Gardner, H., *The Unschooled Mind: How Children Think and How Schools Should Teach*, HarperCollins Publishers, New York, 1992.

Jennings, P., "Common Miracles," ABC News Special on education in the United States and theory of multiple intelligences.

Engaging Messages—Session 2

The following short digests share research findings related to the information presented in Session 2: How Students Learn Best. These are best used *after* Session 2 has been presented. Some schools put one engaging message in each weekly bulletin. Parents come to expect and look forward to learning something about what research studies have found. Other schools promote attendance at future sessions by sharing some of what was learned at the previous session. Even if you don't present Session 2, these engaging messages can be successfully used.

Research shows that active learning is best.

While reading and listening play a role in learning, there is overwhelming evidence that lasting learning and retention of information require that students interact with materials and ideas. An effective teacher is one that involves students in learning by doing, working in groups, discussing, writing, and reflecting, in addition to reading and listening.

Research shows that true understanding goes beyond vocabulary.

Facts and formulas are important in math and science. However, true understanding involves a much deeper approach to learning about concepts. Learning concepts takes longer than rote memorization. Effective teachers seek to present topics in greater depth in order to deepen student understanding.

Research shows that there are recognized phases of learning.

Students need chances to explore phenomena and ideas, receive information, apply what they have learned to new situations, and investigate their own questions. Effective teachers know how to sequence these types of activities so that students learn best.

Research shows that students of different ages have different needs.

Younger students need lots of free exploration and experiential learning opportunities. Older students are more capable of abstract thinking and of applying what they have learned to more complex situations. Research shows that they still need direct interaction with materials. Effective teachers know how to provide students of different ages with the experiences they need.

Research shows that a balanced diet of learning experiences is healthiest!

There's a diverse menu of learning experiences available—hands-on experiments, reading an article, listening to a parent talk about science in his or her career, making a model of the solar system, writing a letter to Bill Gates about a new invention, watching a video, acting out a chemical process, or working together on group presentations are just a few examples. It is good for *all* children to experience *all* approaches to learning. Most educators, like nutritionists, recommend a balanced diet. An effective teacher provides a balance of different learning approaches.

More than one way of being intelligent?

Harvard psychologist Howard Gardner argues that intelligence has to do with the capacity for solving problems and the human ability to create in a complex real-life setting. Taking into account the findings of modern brain science and psychology, Gardner put forward his theory of "multiple intelligences." It suggests that humans have at least seven different kinds of intelligence, including linguistic intelligence, logical-mathematical intelligence, spatial intelligence, bodily-kinesthetic intelligence, musical intelligence, interpersonal intelligence, and intrapersonal intelligence. As Gardner has been quoted as saying, "It's not how smart you are, but *how* you are smart!" It is broadly recognized that IQ tests and other traditional standardized tests measure only a few of these intelligences.

Session 3:
Testing: Knowing What Your Child Knows

Overview

In this workshop, the presenter provides participants with information about testing and assessment. They learn how this area of education has changed since the time they were children, and how they as parents can use some of these newer principles and practices to support their own children's learning. Participants gain a critical sense concerning what they read in the newspaper reports about students' math and science achievement.

The session begins with a discussion about the value of the two kinds of driving tests given at the Department of Motor Vehicles—a multiple choice test about the laws related to driving and a performance test in which a person must actually drive. Groups discuss which test is most important, and how they might feel knowing that a new driver had only been tested in **one** of these ways. This leads to the conclusion that different kinds of tests test for different kinds of knowledge—and both kinds are important. Participants learn that current educational practice strives for a balance of a variety of testing methods. The presenter goes on to introduce the broader concept of assessment (which includes a wide variety of methods for assessing students' knowledge).

The presenter communicates another current educational practice—that student progress should be continuously assessed in small ways throughout a unit of study, rather than solely during tests that happen at the end of each unit. Good teachers assess student knowledge regularly in the course of class and homework. This provides the teacher with timely information about what specific learning needs the student and the class have so the learning opportunities can be adjusted appropriately. Participants learn that in a more informal way, parents can also do this.

The presenter explains the relationship of assessment to curriculum and instruction, and points out that assessment information is important to different audiences for different reasons (teacher, student, parent, school, community, nation).

To gain some firsthand experience, the group participates in an abbreviated learning activity (somewhat as students would). After this short learning experience, they are given a collection of actual student work from two different tests: one is a multiple choice test; the other is a performance test. They work in small groups to see what they can learn about students' knowledge by examining the student work. The whole group discusses the strengths and weaknesses of each method.

Many schools have found this session to be particularly powerful in the spring as teachers and students prepare for standardized testing.

The presenter concludes the discussion by presenting a continuum of learning—from mastery of factual information to the understanding of complex concepts and application of thinking skills. They see how different assessment methods are appropriate depending on the type of knowledge a teacher wants to assess. The limits and benefits of standardized testing are briefly discussed. Parents take home information about strategies they can use to support the establishment of high standards for their own child's school work; ways to work with teachers to support a child's development; and questions to consider when reading the results of testing in the newspaper.

The workshop ends with an optional presentation about standards and standards-based reform and a brief (and reassuring) message about the academic achievement of today's students. This last ten-minute optional ending to the session provides additional information for groups who have digested the main portion of the session. Many groups are hungry for this additional information and ready for it at this time. Other groups may benefit from hearing it at another time. If you have an "experienced" audience, that moves more quickly through earlier portions, you might want to plan to present this additional ten-minute portion within the 75 minutes of this session. Or you can play it by ear, and continue on if you have time and the group has interest. Our field test experience indicated that some audiences need this extra amount of information.

Extending the impact of this session

This session will be valuable to participants in helping them: develop a more current and complex understanding of the issues around testing and assessment; understand some of the educational "jargon" that gets used; feel confident in informally assessing their child's own knowledge and understanding; and then use that information in a constructive way.

To the extent that the session could be "customized" to a particular school's situation, its value will be greatly extended. For instance, if a school has a particular assessment system in place, such as a portfolio system, or standards-based report cards, then mention of that system would be very valuable. Distributing a take-home handout about your school's assessment practices that parents could read at home would be ideal. Information about specific standardized tests given in your district, as well as copies of district or state mathematics and science standards, could also be distributed at the end of the session, providing parents access to information that they don't often have. If possible, use this session as a key step in the important process by which teachers, principals, parents, and other adult caregivers communicate with each other about the educational practices in place at their school.

Time Frame

Total Workshop: 75 minutes
   Introduction (10 minutes)
   Introducing the Horse Race Game (5 minutes)
   Playing and Debriefing the Horse Race Game (15 minutes)
   What Did Students Learn? (15 minutes)
   Reflection and Conclusion (15 minutes)
   Optional: Standards-Based Reform and Are Our Students
     Falling Behind? (10 minutes—note: groups that skip this
     portion are happy for the extra discussion time in earlier
     portions of the session)
   Conclusion (5 minutes)

What You Need

For the presenter:
- ❑ 12 beans or other small counters
  (large lima beans, cubes, or chips work well as counters)
- ❑ 2 dice
- ❑ 1 each of the following overhead transparencies
  (masters on pages 150–168):
  - 1. Goals for the Session
  - 2. Current Practice and Understanding
  - 3. Relationship between Assessment/Instruction/Curriculum
  - 4. Multiple Purposes of Assessment
  - 5. Horse Race Game Board
  - 6. Class Graph
  - 7. Keeping Track
  - 8. How Many Ways?
  - 9. blank Horse Race Quiz
  - 10. blank Letter to a Jockey
  - 11. Analyze Two Kinds of Student Work
  - 12. Letter to a Jockey Scoring Guide
  - 13. Criterion-referenced vs. Norm-referenced
  - 14. Sample Student Rubric
  - 15. Full Range of Learning
  - 16. Bring a Critical Sense to What You Read in the News
  - 17. Standards-Based Reform
  - 18. Why It's Not So Simple
  - 19. New Challenges Schools Face
- ❑ overhead projector
- ❑ extension cord (optional)
- ❑ 1 large-tipped marker
- ❑ 1 sheet of butcher paper or large graph paper
- ❑ masking tape
- ❑ several sheets of self adhesive ("sticky") dots
  (approximately ½" in diameter)

For each participant:

❑ 1 of the following on-table handout:
  • Two Kinds of Tests (master on page 169)
❑ 1 of each of the following take-home handouts:
  • 1. Ways to Help Your Child Achieve High Standards for his/her Work (master on pages 170–172)
  • 2. Don't Believe Everything You Read in the News (master on pages 173–174)
  • 3. Assessing Your Coaching Skills (master on page 175)
  • 4. Test-Taking (master on pages 176–178)
  • 5. Session 3: Research References (master on pages 179–181)

For each pair of participants:

❑ 2 dice
❑ 1 Horse Race Game Board (master on page 154)
❑ 12 beans or other small counters
❑ 1 plastic bag or other small container for the counters

For each group of 4–6 participants:

❑ 2 manila folders
❑ 2 sets of student work: 1 set of the Horse Race Quiz student work (masters on pages 142–145) and 1 set of the Letter to a Jockey student work (masters on pages 146–149)

Getting Ready

Before the Day of the Workshop

1. Duplicate handouts. Decide which take-home handouts you would like to make available to participants. For each participant, duplicate one copy of the on-table handout and whichever of the five take-home handouts you have decided to use.

2. Make overhead transparencies. Make one of each of the 19 overhead transparencies.

3. Make student work folders. Duplicate one copy of the following student work for each group of 4–6 participants:

  • Horse Race Quiz student work
  • Letter to a Jockey student work

For each group of 4–6 participants, prepare two labeled folders containing the student work, one labeled "Horse Race Quiz" and the other labeled "Letter to a Jockey."

4. Make Horse Race Game Boards. Duplicate a copy of the Horse Race Game Board for each pair of participants.

5. Make butcher paper class graph. Make a class graph on a large piece of butcher paper or graph paper. Label one axis with numbers 1–12 for each of the horses. Label the other axis "Number of Wins."

Immediately Before the Workshop

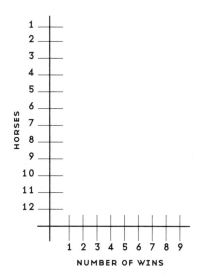

1. Set up the room. Arrange the room so that groups of 4–6 participants can sit at a table together. If you are in a classroom, move desks together to make "tables." Tables should be oriented so that all of the table groups can join a large group discussion, and see what's projected on the overhead.

2. Set up overhead projector. Set up overhead projector at the front of the room near where you will stand.

3. Post class graph. Use masking tape to post the butcher paper class graph in a location where all will be able to see. Set the self adhesive dots near by.

4. Set out on-table handout. Place one copy of the handout, Two Kinds of Tests at each seat, so parents will have something to look at when they first arrive.

5. Have materials for Horse Race demonstration on hand. Place the materials you will use for the Horse Race demonstrations (12 counters and a pair of dice) next to the overhead projector.

6. Have overhead transparencies on hand. Place the overhead transparencies (in numbered order) next to the overhead projector.

7. Assemble remaining workshop materials. Have easily accessible all of the remaining workshop materials:

- dice
- containers of counters
- Horse Race Game Boards
- folders of student work
- take–home handouts

Introduction (10 minutes)

1. Introduce yourself. Introduce yourself and the context of the workshop. Tell them that this session for parents is intended to: a) present what research says about the topic of testing and assessment; and b) provide a forum for discussion about these important educational topics. While this session was designed from the perspective of mathematics and science, and elementary-aged students, most of what will be presented can be generalized to all of learning.

Some parents may be interested in pursuing educational research findings on testing and assessment in more detail. A Research Reference list is provided for this and the other two presentations included in this guide. You may want to mention this to parents up front.

Point out that an hour and fifteen minutes is not long to accomplish the goals of the workshop, and that you have a tight schedule planned. In order to be able to end on time, you will appreciate their cooperation and attention in the workshop.

2. **Outline goals for the day.** Show overhead transparency #1.

Goals for the Session

- Learn about current principles and practices in testing/assessment

- Show how some of these principles and practices can be used informally to assist our children's own learning

(• Discuss the role of standardized testing.)

Explain that the primary goal of today's session is to have a chance to compare the kinds of testing methods that were commonly used in schools when we were young with some of the newer kinds of assessment, and to know what each kind of information tells us about our children's knowledge and progress. Point out that this is where you will spend most of your time.

A second goal of today's session is to help them, as parents, learn how they can use some of these principles and practices to set high work standards for their children. This is the focus of the handouts and is the practical advice they will get.

At the end of the session you will talk a little bit about standardized tests. (If you are presenting the optional ending section, mention that you will also talk a little bit about the role of standards and all of our fear that our children are falling behind.) We certainly read a lot about this in the newspapers. This is not the focus of the session but a natural topic to touch on at the end.

3. **Briefly discuss the DMV testing example.** Begin by referring to the Two Kinds of Tests handout that is at their tables. Ask participants to spend just a few minutes, in groups of 4–6, discussing the two questions at the bottom of the handout. After several minutes, get the group's attention. Ask for several volunteers to share some of what was discussed in their group.

4. Different kinds of tests assess for different kinds of knowledge. Summarize by saying that each kind of test is more appropriate for finding out a different kind of knowledge. In the case of driving, it is hard to imagine not testing in both ways, for both kinds of knowledge. Show overhead transparency #2.

Current Practice and Understanding

· Different kinds of "tests" assess for different kinds of knowledge.

· Create a balance of different kinds of tests so that we can test for a broader range of student knowledge.

· All forms of "tests" are currently referred to more generally as "assessment."

· Assessment should occur before, during, and after learning.

---

5. Balance of testing methods. Say that one of the current practices in education, new since when we were children, is to create a balance of different kinds of tests so that we can test for a broader range of student knowledge. For instance, it's important to find out that children know their math facts (like driving laws); it's equally important to find out that children know how to think critically and solve complex problems (like driving itself).

6. Defining assessment. Say that all the different kinds of tests are currently referred to more generally as "assessment." This is the first of the educational jargon words that you will define today.

7. Continuous assessment. Mention that another current practice in education is for assessment to occur continuously in small ways throughout a unit, rather than only through a long test at the end of a unit. This ensures that information learned through assessment informs the teacher of how best to modify the learning experiences to address areas students are not mastering. It also gives the teacher a fuller picture of each child's abilities and needs. A good teacher is constantly assessing students' progress through daily and weekly home and class assignments, using informal and formal opportunities for assessment. It's not useful to know what you didn't learn at the end of the unit, when you're ready to move on. This information is needed when there is still time to address it.

8. Share relationship between Assessment/ Instruction/ Curriculum. Explain that historically testing was used as a way to select the best students to go on to a very limited number of spots in secondary and post-secondary education. The IQ test was originally developed to choose the best and the brightest to go on to

Parents sometimes wonder where the "tests" are nowadays. Because teachers focus on using a variety of methods to inform them about students' progress, it's not always clear what the test is and when it is occurring. Modern "tests" don't always look like tests.

college. In a situation of limited educational resources, this made sense. However educational resources are no longer as limited. Thus the purpose of assessment needs to change.

Show overhead transparency #3.

Relationship between Assessment/Instruction/Curriculum

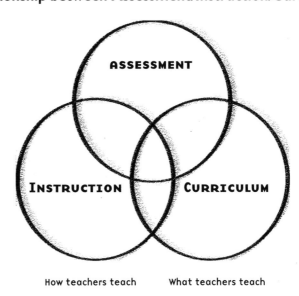

How teachers teach   What teachers teach

Quickly define two more educational jargon words: instruction (how a teacher teaches) and curriculum (what a teacher teaches). Explain that assessment provides important feedback to a teacher about instruction (how she should teach) and curriculum (what she should teach). A good teacher modifies what and how she teaches according to what her students have learned.

9. Share multiple purposes of assessment. Show overhead transparency #4.

Multiple Purposes of Assessment

Assessment ————————————————> Teacher

Assessment ————————————————> Student

Assessment ————————————————> Parent

Assessment ————————————————> School

Assessment ————————————————> Community

Assessment ————————————————> Nation

Say that assessment information is important for the teacher, the student, the parent, the school, the community, and the nation.

Point out that you've already discussed how a **teacher** uses assessment information to measure progress and inform her future actions.

Students need assessment information so they can know what they know and where they need to focus their efforts. Providing assessment information to students helps them internalize standards.

Parents want assessment information in order to be informed of how their child is progressing and how they can be of assistance.

Schools, communities, and the nation need assessment information to know how our students measure up to standards and to other students. It informs where help and additional resources are needed.

The kind of assessment a teacher uses depends on the use of the information—who it is for. Different kinds of assessment situations are better for providing different kinds of information.

Introducing the Horse Race Game (5 minutes)

1. Introduce the activity. Explain that they will participate in a shortened version of a math activity—just enough to provide the common experience of a particular learning activity. Then as a group, they'll focus on the way students' knowledge was assessed, and what insights one can gain by examining student work.

Provide the context for the activity—it's a mathematics activity for 3rd–6th graders from a unit on probability. Tell them it's called, the "Horse Race" activity and that it uses dice.

2. Explain the rules. Show overhead transparency #5.

Sometimes parents wonder whether a game is a valid educational experience. If this should come up, be prepared to reassure the group that games can provide an excellent grounding in mathematics content. As they will see, the Horse Race Game involves students in learning key concepts in probability.

Horse Race ! GAME BOARD

Quickly put a counter on each horse. Explain how the horses move across the track. After a player rolls the pair of dice, he moves the horse whose number is the sum of the dice ahead ONE space. For example, if a six and a three are rolled, the player moves Horse #9 **one space** forward. The horse that crosses the finish line first wins. Emphasize that it is a race between horses, not players.

In many board games, a roll of "4" results in moving a game piece forward 4 spaces. Make sure to emphasize that in this game, a roll of a certain number causes the horse with that number to move forward ONE space.

3. Demonstrate the game on the overhead. Select two participants to model taking turns rolling the dice and moving the appropriate horses. Don't try to finish the game. Just play long enough that everyone understands how to play. This might be just 4 or 5 moves.

4. Explain the class graph. Before setting the participants loose to play their own games, show how they should record the number of the winning horse with a sticky dot on the class graph that you have posted. Tell them that as soon as they finish one game, they should come up and mark their winning horse on the class graph.

Playing and Debriefing the Horse Race Game (15 minutes)

1. Have them begin the game. Distribute game boards, counters, and dice and have them begin. Let them know they will not have as long to play as students, yet they should try to play as many games as they can in the next 5 minutes.

2. Keep the group moving. While playing the game is pleasurable, it is not the goal of the day, so it's important that you keep the session moving. After they have had about 5 minutes to play, let the group know that they should finish the game they are on, and post their results on the class graph.

3. Debrief the activity. Get the group's attention. Show overhead transparency #6.

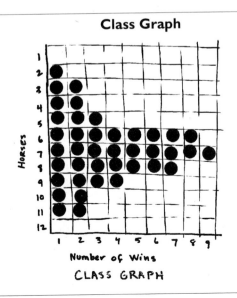

Class Graph

CLASS GRAPH

Explain that students would get to play repeatedly and would generate a set of results like this. Ask:

- What patterns do you notice?

- Why do you think a pattern occurs?

4. Show <u>students'</u> next steps. Tell them that students have the chance to investigate the reason for the pattern.

Important note: Don't attempt to actually lead the participants through steps a. and b., but rather share with them that this is what students do.

a. First show overhead transparency #7 and note how students use this to figure out how many ways there are to get each number with two dice.

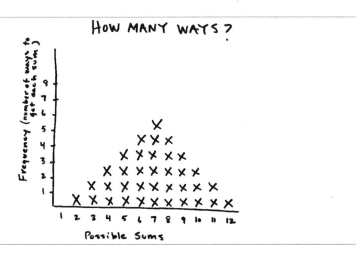

b. Then show overhead transparency #8 and show how students discover the most probable outcomes—7, then 6 or 8.

How Many Ways?

You may want to point out that the process of making meaning of the game experience is key to cementing the learning that occurs.

What Did Students Learn? (15 minutes)

1. Two different "tests." Tell the group that you have actual student work from two different ways of assessing what students learned from playing the Horse Race game but first they'll look at two methods of assessment.

2. Describe the traditional assessment method. Show overhead transparency #9.

Horse Race Quiz

1. With two dice, the most likely number(s) to roll is:
   (circle 1 or more)

       a. 5   d. 8
       b. 7   e. 1
       c. 12   f. 6

2. With two dice, the second most likely number(s) to roll is:
   (circle 1 or more)

       a. 5   d. 8
       b. 7   e. 1
       c. 12   f. 6

3. With two dice, the least likely number to roll is:
   (circle 1 or more)

       a. 5   d. 8
       b. 7   e. 1
       c. 12   f. 6

4. Horse #7 is likely to win because 7 is a lucky number.
       True   False

5. Horse #7 is likely to win because it is in the middle of the numbers.
       True   False

6. Horse #7 is likely to win because it has the highest probability of being rolled.
       True   False

7. Horse #7 is likely to win because it is the sum of 4 and 3.
       True   False

8. Horse #7 is likely to win because it is the sum of 5 and 2.
       True   False

9. How can you be sure which horse is most likely to win?
   (circle the best answer)
           a. it depends which number is luckiest
           b. by playing the game lots of times to see what happens
           c. by knowing the number of different ways you can get each horse's number
           d. it depends how good you are at playing the game
           e. different horses are likely to win on different days

---

Comment that this series of **multiple choice questions** represents one way of finding out what students learned. It is a way that all of us are familiar with, as it is the traditional method that has long been used to test knowledge.

3. Describe the newer assessment method. Show overhead transparency #10 and describe what students were asked to do.

Letter to a Jockey

Write a letter to a jockey and suggest which horses should be first and second choices to ride. Be sure to explain why you've made your recommendation. Drawings and diagrams in your letter will help the jockey understand.

Explain that this is a type of **performance test.** Asking students to write about what they know is currently a common method for assessing student knowledge.

4. Introduce their task. Tell the participants that you will give them two folders; one with student work from the Horse Race Quiz; one with student work from the Letter to a Jockey task. Ask them to work in groups of 4–6 to look at and discuss the student work in each folder. Ask them to focus on what they can tell about what students learned by looking at the student work. Show overhead #11.

Analyze Two Kinds of Student Work

1. Read and discuss the student work in each folder.

2. What does each assessment tell you about the student's level of knowledge? What does it not tell you?

---

5. Have groups begin discussing. Distribute the two student work folders to each group. Let them know they will have about 5–10 minutes to discuss what the student work tells them about what the students learned.

Reflection and Conclusion (15 minutes)

1. Lead a whole group discussion about the student work. Get the whole group's attention. Ask:

- What were you able to learn from looking at the student work from the Horse Race Quiz? from the Letter to a Jockey?
- What were the strengths of each assessment method?
- What were the weaknesses of each method?

Note: The "probability concepts" referred to on the transparency are those the participants have just been introduced to by the game and especially as shown on the Keeping Track and How Many Ways? transparencies. If two standard dice are rolled, some numbers will come up more often because there are more ways to create these sums on the dice. The number 7 is the most likely result because there are six combinations that can add up to 7 (out of 36 possible results). The numbers 6 and 8 are next likely to result, as five possible combinations can add up to both 6 and 8. For the same reason, numbers such as 2 and 12 are less likely to result from the roll of two dice.

2. Scoring tests. Mention that often people are concerned about how newer assessment methods can be scored objectively. Show overhead transparency #12.

Letter to a Jockey
Scoring Guide

Level Four (highest level of work)
Students selected particular horses and supported their conclusion with an extensive application of probability concepts.

Level Three
Students selected particular horses and supported their conclusion with an analysis of class data and a limited application of probability concepts.

Level Two
Students selected particular horses. They based their recommendation solely on an analysis of class data. They did not include an application of probability concepts.

Level One
Students selected particular horses. They based their recommendations on extraneous factors or the results from the few games they played in pairs. They did not support their conclusion with class data or probability concepts.

Say that this is an example of a scoring guide that a teacher might use to objectively compare open-ended student work to specific, verifiable standards. Scoring guides are sometimes referred to as "rubrics."

Mention that research has shown that when teachers have well-constructed rubrics, and know how to use them, there is a high degree of reliability (agreement) on how to score papers (as high as 90%). While these are a lot of "ifs," in theory this way of assessing student work can be highly objective.

3. Norm-referenced vs. criterion-referenced scoring. Show overhead transparency #13.

Criterion-referenced vs. Norm-referenced

Criterion-referenced scoring:
student work is compared to specific criteria described in a scoring guide

Norm-referenced scoring:
student work is compared to other students' work

Tell the group that two more jargon-laden terms we often hear are norm-referenced and criterion-referenced scoring. This Jockey scoring guide is an example of criterion-reference scoring—where student work is compared to criteria, or standards. Norm-referenced scoring refers to student work as compared to other students' work.

4. Students using rubrics. Show overhead transparency #14.

Sample Student Rubric

Investigation Rubric

1) There is a good investigable question:

❏ Uses available equipment and materials.
❏ Is safe and realistic.
❏ Can be answered with a single investigation (not too big a question).
❏ Is a "measuring" question, a "what-happens-if" question, or a "comparison" question (not a "how" or "why" question).

2) An appropriate kind of investigation was selected:

❏ Decided to do a systematic observation because a "measuring" or "what happens-if" question was chosen.

or

❏ Decided to do an experiment because a "comparison" question was chosen or because we turned another kind of question into a "comparison" question.

3) The investigation is well designed:

For Systematic Observations:
❏ Planned the conditions (variables).
❏ Identified possible outcome variables.
❏ Have clear and careful procedure that takes variables into account.

For Experiments:
❏ Identified test variable.
❏ Controlled variables.
❏ Identified outcome variable.
❏ Have clear and careful procedure that takes variables into account.

4) Careful reasoning is used:

❏ Used data and results to support conclusions.
❏ Suggested a well-reasoned explanation.
❏ Thought through problems and additional questions.

5) Ideas are well-communicated:

❏ Ideas are clearly expressed through writing and diagrams so others can understand your investigation and your reasoning.

Say that it is more and more common for teachers to give students a scoring rubric before they do their work. In this way, students understand the work standards that are expected of them. For these students, the formula for high quality work is not a mystery. This practice also helps students start to internalize the standards for good work.

5. Parents role in helping students know and achieve high standards of work. Tell them that part of their role as a parent in coaching their child on his/her homework, is to help the child know what good work is. Point out that deep down all students want to do good work, but many don't know what good work looks like and how to accomplish it. Sometimes students get into a downward cycle of discouragement and become unwilling to try when they experience repeated failure. Parents can help break this cycle.

Hold up the take-home handout, Ways to Help Your Child Achieve High Standards for his/her Work. Spend just a minute explaining that there is a checklist of things to look for, questions to ask your children to help them begin to assess their own work, and other information about how to encourage and help your child in areas where frustrations exist.

6. Introduce notion of full range of learning. Show overhead transparency #15.

Full Range of Learning

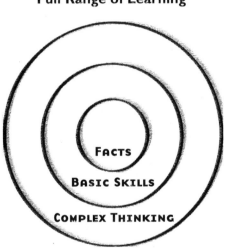

FACTS

BASIC SKILLS

COMPLEX THINKING

Point out that all kinds of learning are important, from mastery of factual information to the understanding of complex concepts and thinking skills. The kind of test or assessment method that is most appropriate depends on the kind of learning a teacher wants to assess.

Let them know that multiple choice and short answer questions are quite adequate for assessing learning related to factual information and basic skills.

Performance tasks, like Letter to a Jockey, are better for assessing the kinds of complex reasoning and mathematical thinking that ensure that a student understands—in this case, understands why there is a greater probability for a certain number to be rolled.

7. Preparation for life. Mention that our education system was crafted in the 1920s, when assembly line and other repetitive work force jobs were more the norm. Only the top of the class was prepared for college and other higher level "thinking" futures. Currently, our work force requires complex thinkers. Even factory workers have a greater role in designing their workdays, understanding what they are doing, and figuring out better ways of doing it. While our country has a long history of focusing on factual knowledge and basic skills, the urgency of preparing all students to be thinkers capable of problem solving and understanding complex concepts is now recognized. We are much newer at teaching complex thinking skills; we are really new at trying to assess for those skills.

8. The issue with standardized tests. Point out that one of the issues raised by many standardized tests, is that most of them are designed to assess factual knowledge and basic skills. The cost-effectiveness of machine-scoring limits the types of assessment that are usually included in these tests. Point out the danger of taking these and other test results out of context; it's always necessary to know what a test is designed to test for before we can conclude more generally about what it means.

9. Assessing the meaning of test results. Show overhead transparency #16.

Bring a Critical Sense to What You Read in the News

- What was the test designed to measure? Factual recall? Complex thinking?

- Were students being tested on what they were taught?

- Was there a connection between what was tested and what state/national standards say is important that students should know?

- Were students tested in a language they understood?

- Was the test measuring rapid recall or thoughtful response?

- How does what was tested relate to desired work force skills?

Tell the group that the second take-home handout you have for them is entitled, Don't Believe Everything You Read in the News. Among other things, it has some questions for you to consider when you read about test results. Mention a few of the questions on the overhead.

Optional: Standards-Based Reform and Are Our Students Falling Behind? (10 minutes)

1. Standardized tests work best when they are based on agreed-upon standards. Show overhead transparency #17.

Standards-Based Reform

Standards

↓

Assessment

↓

Curriculum

Say that many of them might have heard another jargon term: standards-based reform. Explain that standards-based reform refers to a situation where there are agreed-upon standards about what students should know, there are standardized tests that test for that knowledge, and a standards-based curriculum that teaches what's in the standards.

In theory, this makes infinite sense, and seems very simple.

2. Why it's not so simple. Show overhead transparency #18.

Why It's Not So Simple

Which standards should be used?

What's the mix of knowledge and reasoning?

Which knowledge?

For which students?

What role should standards play?

Explain that for standards-based reform to work, there needs to be excellent and agreed-upon standards about what children should know. This has been harder than it seems for the community to agree on.

Briefly talk through each of the questions on the overhead, explaining what the issues are.

Which standards should be used? Does a school district rely on national standards, state standards, or district standards? This would be easier if all of these were related. In the case of some states, such as California and Virginia, the state standards are significantly different from the national standards.

What's the mix of knowledge and reasoning? Should standards be based on mostly things which must be memorized or mostly things which require reasoning? This is a major difference in different sets of standards.

Which knowledge? Should students know the state capitals? About biotechnology? About why earthquakes occur? About the Periodic Table? The amount of knowledge there is in any one subject area is so great and increasing so rapidly that it is necessary to pick and choose what's important. Most standards include much more than a teacher could ever teach in a year. There has also been great controversy over those standards that have attempted to eliminate specific areas of knowledge.

For which students? Should standards be written so they are attainable by all students? Or should they be challenging so they are attainable by just the best students? The controversy has raged under the guise of low standards vs. elitist standards.

What role should standards play? Should standards be advisory to a school, required by a school, or should they drive academic advancement? This boils down to whether anyone is accountable for standards, and if so, whether it should be schools, teachers, or the student him- or herself. "High stakes" standards are what's referred to when a school's funding is dependent on how its students perform on standardized tests and/or when a student can only advance to the next grade when s/he has demonstrated knowledge of the standards.

The process of attempting to agree on standards has been a highly political process. Especially given our nation's strong culture of autonomy and democracy, the standards battle will continue to be a hard and complex one. This is in sharp contrast to other countries, who set standards relatively easily, without much input or controversy.

Conclude by saying that standards-based reform could be an enlightened path or a regressive path, depending on what you think of the quality of the standards that are driving the process.

3. Are our kids falling behind? Refer to the common messages we read in the press: American students are way behind our international counterparts, and current students are way behind where we were (20 and 30 years ago) when we were in school.

Important Note: Educational reform in our country can be characterized by a series of pendulum swings. One can go back over the past 75–100 years and note how the favored "solutions" to the "problems" of education have changed every 10–20 years, frequently alternating between one extreme and another. It is important to realize what it means to students, teachers, and schools when the policy pendulum swings back and forth. Particularly when policy changes are accompanied with accountability measures, schools and teachers are jerked back and forth as they attempt to comply with what are sometimes opposite approaches. Policy is driven by public opinion. In the long run, parents can play a role in changing the drastic swings by advocating for a more balanced approach. In the short run, parents' sensitivity to the difficult and complex situation in which schools and teachers must operate will help create a more supportive environment for improving education for our children.

Mention that a group of scientists from Sandia Lab (not educators) spent several years comparing every measurable indicator of academic success: graduation rates, SAT scores, the number of students going on to secondary education, etc. This Sandia report came to the conclusion that, on every single measure, today's students are equal to or better than students 30 years ago. They point out some of the problems with how the press has distorted data.

4. Why this is controversial. Needless to say, this is a controversial report. People who don't like current educational approaches don't want it shown that they are effective. People who are involved with current approaches don't want the conclusion that everything is fine and that more money isn't needed.

This is not to say that there are not serious problems in our educational system that need attention. This is just a note of reassurance—that the sky is not falling.

5. New challenges schools face. Show overhead transparency #19.

New Challenges Schools Face

1) Social conditions

2) More critical thinkers are needed in the workforce

Point out that there are at least two significant differences in the challenges that schools now face, as compared to 30 years ago.

1) It used to be that gum chewing and running in the hallways were serious offenses; now the social problems of violence and drugs have entered our schools.

2) As mentioned earlier, we need more critical thinkers in the workforce now.

In spite of these increased challenges, the academic achievement of today's students is equal to or better than in the past.

Mention that the Research References page you will be distributing has the references for both the Sandia Report and some other articles written about it.

6. International comparisons. As for international comparisons, it is true that our students don't do as well in science and math at kindergarten through 12th grade. However, the balance shifts at and after the post-secondary level. The U.S. science, technology, and math research work force is the strongest in the world. There are more Nobel Laureates per capita in our country than any other. This in turn prompts the question of what these international tests *aren't* testing.

Conclusion (5 minutes)

1. Reiterate the key point. Say that in some ways today's session just scratches the surface of testing and assessment and how it fits into the educational movement today. Emphasize that the handouts are focused on practical advice.

2. Distribute take-home sheets. Set the take-home handouts and the Research Reference list on a table so parents can take what they'd like when they leave.

3. If you're planning to present other sessions, let them know when and where, and encourage them to bring other parents.

4. Be sure to thank all the participants for coming and for the ideas and comments they've shared. If you have a feedback or evaluation form for the participants, urge them to complete it so presentations can be improved in the future.

Going Further

1. Spend time showing parents how to interpret the results of the standardized test used in your school district. Use examples of last year's test results. Explain concepts like percentile, mean, and median. If available, share your district's test results broken out by different variables such as, gender, language group, socioeconomic background, school, etc. If possible, share sample test questions from past versions of actual tests.

2. Provide information about how to discuss assessment techniques with teachers in ways that are tactful and constructive and yet raise whatever concerns a parent might have.

3. Some of the take-home handouts would provide great read-and-discuss situations for groups of four participants. For instance the handouts on Test-Taking and Ways to Help Your Child Achieve High Standards for his/her Work are ones that participants often want a chance to discuss.

Horse Race Quiz

1. With two dice, the most likely number(s) to roll is:
   (circle 1 or more)
   - a. 5
   - b. (7)
   - c. 12
   - d. (8)
   - e. 1
   - f. 6

2. With two dice, the second most likely number(s) to roll is:
   (circle 1 or more)
   - a. (5)
   - b. 7
   - c. 12
   - d. 8
   - e. 1
   - f. (6)

3. With two dice, the least likely number to roll is:
   (circle 1 or more)
   - a. 5
   - b. 7
   - c. (12)
   - d. 8
   - e. (1)
   - f. 6

4. Horse #7 is likely to win because 7 is a lucky number.
   True (False)

5. Horse #7 is likely to win because it is in the middle of the numbers.
   (True) False

6. Horse #7 is likely to win because it has the highest probability of being rolled.
   True (False)

7. Horse #7 is likely to win because it is the sum of 4 and 3.
   (True) False

8. Horse #7 is likely to win because it is the sum of 5 and 2.
   (True) False

9. How can you be sure which horse is most likely to win?
   (circle the best answer)
   a. it depends which number is luckiest
   b. by playing the game lots of times to see what happens
   c. by knowing the number of different ways you can get each horse's number
   d. it depends how good you are at playing the game
   e. (different horses are likely to win on different days)

Horse Race Quiz

1. With two dice, the most likely number(s) to roll is:
   (circle 1 or more)

   a. 5   (d.) 8
   b.(7)   e. 1
   c. 12   f. 6

2. With two dice, the second most likely number(s) to roll is:
   (circle 1 or more)

   a. 5   d. 8
   (b.) 7   e. 1
   c. 12   f. 6

3. With two dice, the least likely number to roll is:
   (circle 1 or more)

   a. 5   d. 8
   b. 7   e.(1)
   c. 12   f. 6

4. Horse #7 is likely to win because 7 is a lucky number.
   (True) False

5. Horse #7 is likely to win because it is in the middle of the numbers.
   (True) False

6. Horse #7 is likely to win because it has the highest probability of being rolled.
   True (False)

7. Horse #7 is likely to win because it is the sum of 4 and 3.
   (True) False

8. Horse #7 is likely to win because it is the sum of 5 and 2.
   (True) False

9. How can you be sure which horse is most likely to win?
   (circle the best answer)

   a. it depends which number is luckiest
   b.(by playing the game lots of times to see what happens)
   c. by knowing the number of different ways you can get each horse's number
   d. it depends how good you are at playing the game
   e. different horses are likely to win on different days

Horse Race Quiz

1. With two dice, the most likely number(s) to roll is:
   (circle 1 or more)
   - a. 5
   - **b. 7** *(circled)*
   - c. 12
   - d. 8
   - e. 1
   - f. 6

2. With two dice, the second most likely number(s) to roll is:
   (circle 1 or more)
   - a. 5
   - b. 7
   - c. 12
   - **d. 8** *(circled)*
   - e. 1
   - **f. 6** *(circled)*

3. With two dice, the least likely number to roll is:
   (circle 1 or more)
   - a. 5
   - b. 7
   - c. 12
   - d. 8
   - **e. 1** *(circled)*
   - f. 6

4. Horse #7 is likely to win because 7 is a lucky number.
   True **(False)** *(circled)*

5. Horse #7 is likely to win because it is in the middle of the numbers.
   True **(False)** *(circled)*

6. Horse #7 is likely to win because it has the highest probability of being rolled.
   (True) *(circled)* False

7. Horse #7 is likely to win because it is the sum of 4 and 3.
   True **(False)** *(circled)*

8. Horse #7 is likely to win because it is the sum of 5 and 2.
   True **(False)** *(circled)*

9. How can you be sure which horse is most likely to win?
   (circle the best answer)
   - a. it depends which number is luckiest
   - b. by playing the game lots of times to see what happens
   - **c. by knowing the number of different ways you can get each horse's number** *(circled)*
   - d. it depends how good you are at playing the game
   - e. different horses are likely to win on different days

Horse Race Quiz

1. With two dice, the most likely number(s) to roll is:
   (circle 1 or more)

   a. 5   d. 8
   ✓b. 7   e. 1
   c. 12   f. 6

2. With two dice, the second most likely number(s) to roll is:
   (circle 1 or more)

   ✓a. 5   d. 8
   b. 7   e. 1
   c. 12   f. 6

3. With two dice, the least likely number to roll is:
   (circle 1 or more)

   a. 5   d. 8
   b. 7   ✓e. 1
   c. 12   f. 6

4. Horse #7 is likely to win because 7 is a lucky number.
   True (False)

5. Horse #7 is likely to win because it is in the middle of the numbers.
   True (False)

6. Horse #7 is likely to win because it has the highest probability of being rolled.
   (True) False

7. Horse #7 is likely to win because it is the sum of 4 and 3.
   True (False)

8. Horse #7 is likely to win because it is the sum of 5 and 2.
   True (False)

9. How can you be sure which horse is most likely to win?
   (circle the best answer)

   a. it depends which number is luckiest
   b. by playing the game lots of times to see what happens
   ✓c. by knowing the number of different ways you can get each horse's number
   d. it depends how good you are at playing the game
   e. different horses are likely to win on different days

Dear Jockey,
You should choose horse 7, because it has six ways to win here they are.
WAYS TO GET SEVEN IN DICE

You should pick 6 or 8 for your second choice because there are five ways to get those numbers. Here they are.
WAYS TO GET EIGHT IN DICE

WAYS TO GET SIX IN DICE

Sincerely,
Emile

P.S. If you do this you'll be this.

Dear Jockey,

I think you should pick horse number seven because there are six ways to make seven on two dice. Your next choice should eather be a 6 or 8 because both of them have 5 ways to make themselves. Look at this chart explaining what I just told you.

--- Robert E.

	⚀	⚁	⚂	⚃	⚄	⚅
⚀	2	3	4	5	6	7
⚁	3	4	5	6	7	8
⚂	4	5	6	7	8	9
⚃	5	6	7	8	9	10
⚄	6	7	8	9	10	11
⚅	7	8	9	10	11	12

Dear Jockeys,
    I think you should pick number seven for your first choice. The reson why I think you should is because if you count all the ways how to make seven youll get 6 of them and more often youll get seven. A nother reson is for it is in the middle of all numbers on the horse race. Now for your second choice I would pick 6. For instance it has five ways to make to make it is only one number less than seven. Hope you pick a good horse.

    From
        Kira

Dear Jocky,

I think your first choice of horse whould be horse number 7 beacause on our class graph it shows the results. 7 got 13, 6 got 12, 8 got 5, 9 got 4. Those are your first 4 choices. The last ones are number 4, 5, 3, 2, 1, 10, 11, 12. Those are the worst.

Well, I learned alot about probtlies,

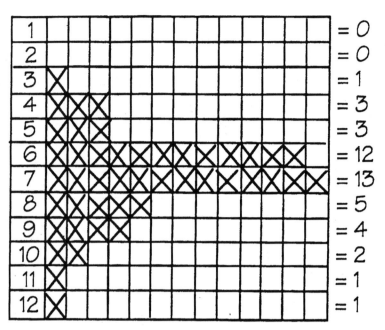

1	= 0
2	= 0
3	= 1
4	= 3
5	= 3
6	= 12
7	= 13
8	= 5
9	= 4
10	= 2
11	= 1
12	= 1

Yours sinserly, Margaret

Dear Jocky,

I think you should pick seven and if you don't get number seven, I would pic number six. I think you should pick seven because seven is my lucky number and I'm rooting for you. And, if you don't get seven, get six because six is an awesome number.
Sincerely, D.J.

Steve

Dear Jocky

I think you should ride number 7 first then 6. I picked thous horses becase number 7 has a good pastern and a good loins and a hock and a good shank and a good fetlock.

Dear jockey,

If I where you, my first choice would be # 7 Because # 7 has the most wins. If you can't be #7, then be #6 because it has the second most wins. I hope you win.

— Robert S.

FiNiSh

7 of 6

Dear Jockey,

I think you should ride on horse number seven first because it has six chances to win and that's more than the eleven other horses. The next horse you should ride on is number six or eight because it has five chances to win and that's more than the nine other horses.
In the all the races, horse number seven still has more chances.
That is why you should ride on those horses.

Sincerely,
Jack L.

Goals for the Session

• Learn about current principles and practices in testing/assessment

• Show how some of these principles and practices can be used informally to assist our children's own learning

(• Discuss the role of standardized testing.)

Current Practice and Understanding

• Different kinds of "tests" assess for different kinds of knowledge.

• Create a balance of different kinds of tests so that we can test for a broader range of student knowledge.

• All forms of "tests" are currently referred to more generally as "assessment."

• Assessment should occur before, during, and after learning.

Relationship between Assessment/Instruction/Curriculum

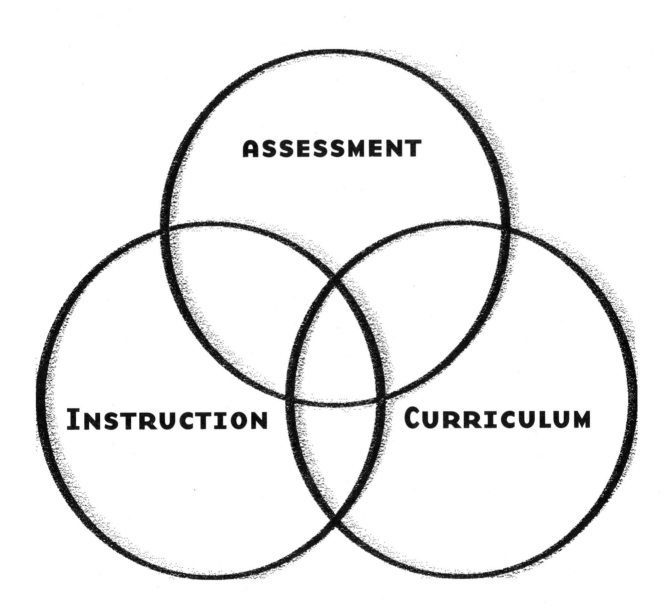

ASSESSMENT

INSTRUCTION

CURRICULUM

How teachers teach   What teachers teach

Multiple Purposes
of Assessment

Assessment ——————————➤ Teacher

Assessment ——————————➤ Student

Assessment ——————————➤ Parent

Assessment ——————————➤ School

Assessment ——————————➤ Community

Assessment ——————————➤ Nation

Horse Race !
GAME BOARD

1							①
2							②
3							③
4							④
5							⑤
6							⑥
7							⑦
8							⑧
9							⑨
10							⑩
11							⑪
12							⑫

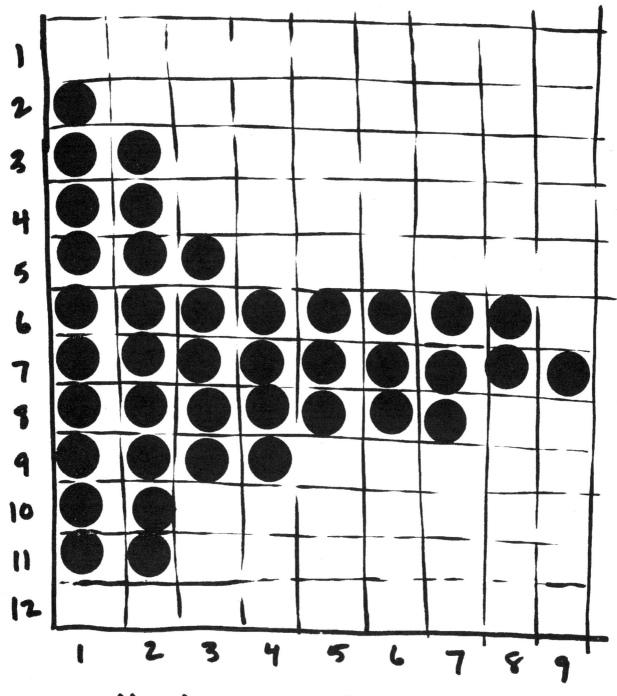

Number of Wins

CLASS GRAPH

Keeping Track

	·	:	∴	::	⁙	⚅
·	2	3	4	5	6	7
:	3	4	5	6	7	8
∴	4	5	6	7	8	9
::	5	6	7	8	9	10
⁙	6	7	8	9	10	11
⚅	7	8	9	10	11	12

HOW MANY WAYS?

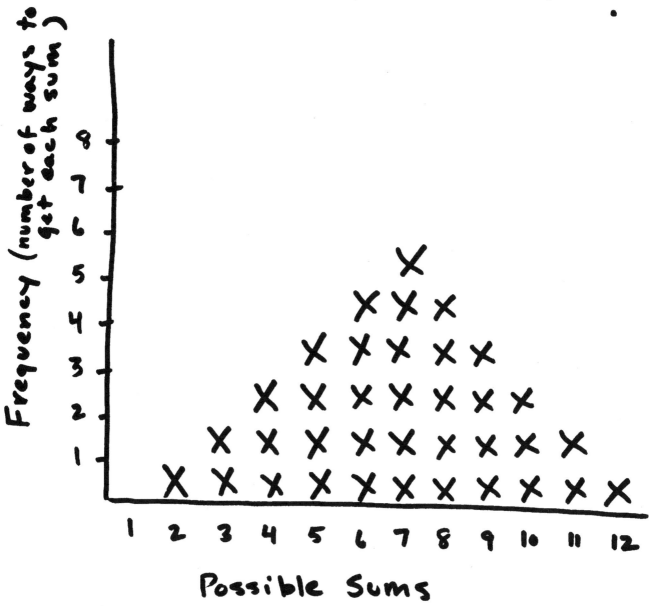

Possible Sums

Horse Race Quiz

1. With two dice, the most likely number(s) to roll is:
   (circle 1 or more)

   a. 5   d. 8

   b. 7   e. 1

   c. 12   f. 6

2. With two dice, the second most likely number(s) to roll is:
   (circle 1 or more)

   a. 5   d. 8

   b. 7   e. 1

   c. 12   f. 6

3. With two dice, the least likely number to roll is:
   (circle 1 or more)

   a. 5   d. 8

   b. 7   e. 1

   c. 12   f. 6

4. Horse #7 is likely to win because 7 is a lucky number.
   True   False

5. Horse #7 is likely to win because it is in the middle of the numbers.
   True   False

6. Horse #7 is likely to win because it has the highest probability of being rolled.
   True   False

7. Horse #7 is likely to win because it is the sum of 4 and 3.
   True   False

8. Horse #7 is likely to win because it is the sum of 5 and 2.
   True   False

9. How can you be sure which horse is most likely to win?
   (circle the best answer)

   a. it depends which number is luckiest

   b. by playing the game lots of times to see what happens

   c. by knowing the number of different ways you can get each horse's number

   d. it depends how good you are at playing the game

   e. different horses are likely to win on different days

Letter to a Jockey

Write a letter to a jockey and suggest which horses should be first and second choices to ride. Be sure to explain why you've made your recommendation. Drawings and diagrams in your letter will help the jockey understand.

Analyze Two Kinds of Student Work

1. Read and discuss the student work in each folder.

2. What does each assessment tell you about the student's level of knowledge? What does it not tell you?

Letter to a Jockey
Scoring Guide

Level Four (highest level of work)

Students selected particular horses and supported their conclusion with an extensive application of probability concepts.

Level Three

Students selected particular horses and supported their conclusion with an analysis of class data and a limited application of probability concepts.

Level Two

Students selected particular horses. They based their recommendation solely on an analysis of class data. They did not include an application of probability concepts.

Level One

Students selected particular horses. They based their recommendations on extraneous factors or the results from the few games they played in pairs. They did not support their conclusion with class data or probability concepts.

Criterion-referenced vs. Norm-referenced

Criterion-referenced scoring: student work is compared to specific criteria described in a scoring guide

Norm-referenced scoring: student work is compared to other students' work

Sample Student Rubric

Investigation Rubric

1) There is a good investigable question:

❑ Uses available equipment and materials.
❑ Is safe and realistic.
❑ Can be answered with a single investigation (not too big a question).
❑ Is a "measuring" question, a "what-happens-if" question, or a "comparison" question (not a "how" or "why" question).

2) An appropriate kind of investigation was selected:

❑ Decided to do a systematic observation because a "measuring" or "what happens-if" question was chosen.

        or

❑ Decided to do an experiment because a "comparison" question was chosen or because we turned another kind of question into a "comparison" question.

3) The investigation is well designed:

For Systematic Observations:
❑ Planned the conditions (variables).
❑ Identified possible outcome variables.
❑ Have clear and careful procedure that takes variables into account.

For Experiments:
❑ Identified test variable.
❑ Controlled variables.
❑ Identified outcome variable.
❑ Have clear and careful procedure that takes variables into account.

4) Careful reasoning is used:

❑ Used data and results to support conclusions.
❑ Suggested a well-reasoned explanation.
❑ Thought through problems and additional questions.

5) Ideas are well-communicated:

❑ Ideas are clearly expressed through writing and diagrams so others can understand your investigation and your reasoning.

Full Range of Learning

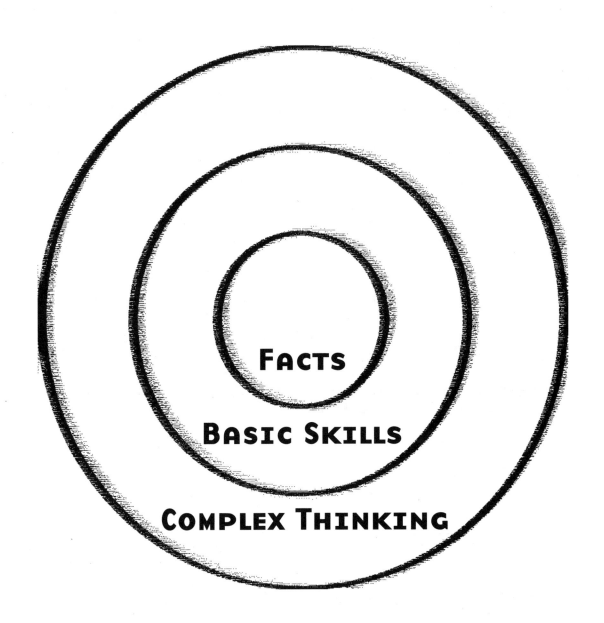

FACTS

BASIC SKILLS

COMPLEX THINKING

Bring a Critical Sense to What You Read in the News

• What was the test designed to measure? Factual recall? Complex thinking?

• Were students being tested on what they were taught?

• Was there a connection between what was tested and what state/national standards say is important that students should know?

• Were students tested in a language they understood?

• Was the test measuring rapid recall or thoughtful response?

• How does what was tested relate to desired work force skills?

Standards-Based Reform

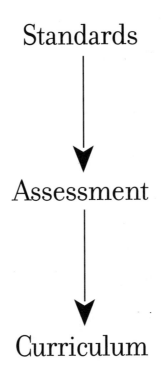

Standards

↓

Assessment

↓

Curriculum

Why It's Not So Simple

Which standards should be used?

What's the mix of knowledge and reasoning?

Which knowledge?

For which students?

What role should standards play?

New Challenges
Schools Face

1) Social conditions

2) More critical thinkers are
   needed in the workforce

Ideas ◄
Suggestions ◄
Resources ◄

that lead to Great Explorations
in Math and Science!

**Sign up
now for a
free subscription
to the *GEMS*
Network News!**

LHS GEMS

LH68
101 Lawrence Hall of Science # 5200

Get Connected!

www.lhs.berkeley.edu/gems

Two Kinds of Tests

After a person learns to drive, he or she goes to the Department of Motor Vehicles to be tested. There, the person takes two different tests to demonstrate his or her capability to be a licensed driver.

One test is a multiple choice test. The person must correctly answer questions about the laws related to driving.

The other test is a performance test. The person must skillfully drive a car in a variety of road situations.

- Which test is most important?

- Would you feel confident in knowing that a new driver had only been tested in one of these ways?

WAYS TO HELP YOUR CHILD ACHIEVE HIGH STANDARDS FOR HIS/HER WORK

Every child wants to succeed! But not all children know what they need to do to be successful. As a parent, you can help your child know how to be successful. Here are some suggestions:

Checking out your child's work: In reviewing your child's school papers or homework, ask yourself questions like:

- Has he answered the question that was asked?
- Does she need to provide a more complete response?
- Do the ideas make sense? Are they presented in a logical order?
- Did she provide an explanation of how she solved the problem?
- Did he explain why he knows something to be true?
- Is there information she doesn't know which is making the task harder?
- Is he holding on to some inaccurate information that is interfering with his understanding?

Questions that can help your child begin to internalize high standards for his/her own work: Some of these questions are also good for you to ask your child as a way of helping with homework. There is lots of evidence that students who know the standards for good work themselves are best able to produce good work. Asking questions like the following can help a child begin to learn these standards. Then, when your children are working on other tasks, they may ask themselves the same kind of questions.

- Explain how you figured that problem out.
- How do you know that is correct?
- Why do you think that? Write your thinking down.
- Can both of these things be true?
- Can you find a better way to convince the reader of your answer?
- Can you make a drawing that shows what you mean?
- Have you labeled your drawing?
- Did you describe the units correctly? (inches, milliliters, meters, teaspoons)
- How is this similar to what you did in class?
- What part is hard for you? How could we make that part easier?
- If a child has an incorrect solution, suggest two or three other solutions and ask them to compare them. Does one look more correct than the others?

Ways to encourage your child: Recognize that improvement takes time and happens most easily in an environment of encouragement and support. Frustration is a predictable and natural phase in learning. Help your child work through her frustration. Focus on one area of improvement at a time. Celebrate your child's progress even when it seems small! Explain that every person has things they can do easily and things that they have to work harder to accomplish. Talk openly about what you perceive to be your child's strengths as well as her challenges. Talk to your child's teacher if you need additional strengths and challenges to add to your list. Share with your child what you perceive as your own strengths and challenges and discuss how you work on improving yourself.

Comparing your child's performance to grade level expectations: Talk to your child's teacher about how his performance compares to other children in the class, in the grade level, the state, the nation. Report cards usually show your child's performance compared to others at the grade level. Sometimes parents' expectations for children's academic performance are unrealistically high; other times parents don't realize that their child lags behind. Keep in mind that children develop at different rates; often time will take care of certain problems. Your child's teacher is likely to recognize when this is the case. Ask for a copy of district, state, or national standards for your child's grade level, or find out where to get a copy. Standardized tests have many shortcomings, but can provide information about your child's performance in areas of basic abilities, usually letting you know if there is either high level achievement, or a serious problem. Use this information, together with your child's report card, in conversations with your child's teacher. Use your own informal assessments of your child's capabilities to advocate for and assist your child's development in those areas of greatest need.

What to do to help your child improve in a certain area: As you get a sense of your child's particular challenge (explaining her thinking, thinking logically, hates to write, doesn't understand what a complete sentence is, doesn't know math facts, doesn't think in an order that makes sense, doesn't take risks, works too fast, etc.), focus your help in this area. Write a note to your child's teacher alerting her to your perception of the problem and asking for specific ways to help your child in this particular area at home. Inquire how the teacher is helping your child in this particular area at school. She may want to schedule a meeting to talk more about it.

Work together to strike a balance: Remember that encouragement and support can set the scene for further progress. At the same time, it is important to have high expectations and make sure your child knows what kind of work meets standards of excellence. Working together, with your child, teachers, and the school, you can help your child improve and advance.

DON'T BELIEVE EVERYTHING YOU READ IN THE NEWS

Bring a critical sense to what you read in the newspapers. When reading about test results, wonder the following:

- What was the test designed to measure? Factual recall? Complex thinking?
- Were students being tested on what they were taught?
- Was there a connection between what was tested and what state or national standards say is important that students should know?
- Were students tested in a language they understood?
- Was the test measuring rapid recall or thoughtful response?
- How does what was tested relate to desired work force skills?

Test results in the news. The results of standardized testing and international comparisons always seem to attract attention—especially when they are shocking! Reporters are often looking for attention grabbing angles so that is how this news is typically framed. It is not uncommon for news reports to make use of simplistic, or highly aggregated data to draw unwarranted conclusions. For instance, an international examination tested students for their knowledge of algebra a year before U.S. students typically study algebra in school. It's not surprising that U.S. students did not test well in algebra! Another recent report about statewide standardized test results spoke alarmingly about students' lack of knowledge as reflected by the below average test scores. Nowhere did it mention that students had 20 minutes to answer 60 questions. Rapid recall and knowledge are not the same, especially for students who are not practiced in test-taking strategy.

The value of standardized test results. When a test is well-designed, focused on highly valued knowledge and skills, and administered in a way to reduce bias, the results can provide very important information. But even then, the cause of a "bad" test result, or even the value of a test result in predicting a student's future success are not at all clear. For instance, it is well-accepted that a high score on the SAT (Scholastic Aptitude Test) is not the best predictor of future success in college. Test results should be considered as one of many things when assessing a student's knowledge and abilities. The purpose of test results should not be to brand a student or a school as "good" or "bad," but rather to know where adjustment in instruction is needed.

Consider the Source. In addition to the sometimes sensationalized and simplistic approach of the media, various interest groups may have reasons to put their own "spin" on interpreting test results. Interpretations of some reports may be slanted in defense of stakeholders in the system, such as administrators, teacher's unions, or the established bureaucracies of state education departments or large districts. Groups that don't like currently accepted approaches to education are definitely motivated to conclude that things are not good enough at present and may emphasize one finding of a test over another. Those who think current approaches make sense, but think education is vastly underfunded might also tend to conclude that things are not good enough, in the hope that more money will be allocated. Even those who feel pleased with the progress made, but hold high standards and want to head off a natural tendency toward complacency may want to send out a somewhat critical message. In a way then, all of these negative conclusions could play a positive role, in that they would support changes in the educational system—but the real question is whether or not the changes they advocate are realistic and based upon needs and factors other than test scores. There are many credible and careful research studies that indicate problems with the U.S. educational system, and there are serious educational challenges, but it is important to find out whether or not a group may have a particular agenda or goal. It is useful to seek out those media reports that provide this level of analysis.

An example of how truth gets distorted. There is a widely publicized decline in average SAT (Scholastic Aptitude Test) scores among United States college-bound high school students since 1975. While this is a correct statement, it distorts the more complex truth of the situation. It turns out that more people in the United States are aspiring to go to college than ever before. Thus more people are taking the SAT test. Of this increasing number of test takers, a greater percentage rank in the bottom half of their high school classes. A study carried out by Sandia National Laboratories[1] compared 1975 to current SAT scores, looking at just those students from the same class rank and gender. It found that when these factors were controlled, the average SAT score for this "traditional test-taking population" actually increased by 30 points.

Don't panic over media reports! As a parent, it is especially difficult not to react with alarm to reports that our students and schools are failing. Be sure to bring a critical sense to what you read and then draw your own conclusions. If you have questions about a test your child took, ask to speak with your principal.

How you can make a difference. It can be frustrating to read about things that relate to our children in the paper, and yet feel helpless in improving the educational system. A tremendous amount of research has been done about whether and how parents can make a difference for students.[2] This research strongly concludes that when parents do these things at home, their children do better in school: provide a special time and place for study; encourage the child daily through discussion; attend to the student's progress in school; encourage the child on any gains; and cooperate with your child's teacher.

---

[1] Carson, Huelskamp, and Woodall, The Sandia Report: "Perspectives on Education in America," in *The Journal of Educational Research*, May/June 1993; Volume 86; Number 5.

[2] Henderson and Berla, *A New Generation of Evidence: The Family is Critical to Student Achievement*, 1994.

ASSESSING YOUR COACHING SKILLS

Parents as coaches play a powerful role in helping children develop good learning skills and attitudes for life-long success. Although you never signed up to be—nor should you be—a school teacher for your child, building a good relationship as collaborators in the learning process can be both productive and enjoyable for parent and child alike.

However, even the most skilled teachers and tutors often have trouble helping their own children with schoolwork. Because we care so much about how our children do in school, it's easy to fall into several dangerous traps. Instead of coaching, we may try to get overly involved, bossy, or demanding. Learning does not need to become a family battle ground.

Next time you coach your child as s/he does homework, reflect on which of the following successful approaches you used. Work on incorporating more and more of these strategies over time.

Mark an "E" for excellent, "S" for satisfactory, or "N" for needs work.

1. I am available to my child.   _____

2. I offer support, not criticism.   _____

3. I focus on effort and improvement
    instead of grades.   _____

4. I don't worry about being an expert.   _____

5. I don't expect perfection.   _____

6. I turn the thinking over to my child.   _____

7. I enjoy coaching my child.   _____

What will you do to improve your coaching next time?

_____

_____

_____

Modified and adapted with permission from: *Helping Your Child Succeed in School: A Guide for Parents of 4 to 14 Year Olds*, by Popkin, Youngs, and Healy, Active Parenting Publishers, Atlanta, Georgia, 1995. Refer to this excellent resource for more in-depth information.

Test-Taking

Test-taking is a skill, one that can be learned just as well as the academic subjects that tests measure. Following are some good tips for helping you and your children develop this skill and some excellent resources on the topic. Not every approach mentioned below is appropriate for every testing situation and every age child, but you and your child will benefit from an overall knowledge of good test-taking. Go over these with your children and work together to adapt these hints to your children's individual learning styles and their situation.

Studying for the Test

- **Studying should begin soon after the school year starts.** Keep notes organized for review and keep up with homework.

- **Listen for hints from the teacher about what will be on the test.** Ask him for hints about where to concentrate your efforts.

- **Determine the most important information in your study materials and learn that first.**

- **Begin your intensive studying early in the afternoon or evening before the day of the test.**

- **Develop a practice test either alone or with a study mate.** You may want to write a list of questions that may appear on your test before you begin intensive studying, so the list can guide you through your studying. Or you might ask a friend to give you a practice test near the end of your studying in order to catch any final items you may have overlooked.

- **Use positive self-talk.** Research shows that students who study and work on their self-confidence perform better than those who study only. For example, thoughts such as "I am well prepared and will do fine on this test" can help maintain a calm and clear mind.

- **Gather all test-taking materials the night before.** Having to borrow a pencil right before the test can break your concentration and get you off to a bad start.

- **Don't stay up too late and eat a good breakfast.** On the morning of the test, you will perform better with a rested mind and an energized body.

Taking the Test

Phase 1: Review the Test

- **First and foremost, read the instructions very carefully and follow the directions exactly.** Missing something here can cost you dramatically. For example, your instructions might ask you to answer one of the following two essay questions; if you missed those instructions, you would waste half your test-taking time writing an unnecessary essay.

- **Quickly read through the entire test, noting which questions are most difficult, which count the most, and which you don't understand.**

- **Ask questions about anything you don't understand.** Shy children may need to practice how to ask for clarification.

- **Budget your time, allowing more time for essay questions.** ("I'll spend 10 minutes on the true/false section, 20 minutes on the multiple choice, and 30 minutes on the essay.")

- **Take a deep breath.** It will help you relax and think more clearly.

Phase 2: Take the Test

- **Answer the easiest questions first.** Not only is this good time management, but it will also build confidence.

- **Go back to the more difficult questions, but don't spend too much time on any one question until you have completed all of the others.**

- **Write clearly.**

- **Pay attention to clues and key words in each question.** For example, some choices in multiple choice questions may be eliminated because they would make the completed sentence grammatically incorrect.

- **Put something down for every question even if you don't know the answer.** You may know more than you think you know. Note: Children may be instructed while taking standardized tests that incorrect answers will cost them more deductions than answers that they have left blank. Make sure you know the exact instructions for each test.

Phase 3: Review

- **Review every item carefully before turning in your test.**
  You may catch a careless error or have a last-minute insight.

- **Use all of the time allowed.** The longer you review your answer, the more chances you have to discover mistakes.

Recommended Resources

Gilbert, Sara, *How to Take Tests*, William Morrow and Company, Inc., New York, 1983.

Gruber, Gary, *Dr. Gruber's Essential Guide to Test Taking for Kids*, William Morrow and Company, Inc., New York, 1986.

Modified and adapted with permission from: *Helping Your Child Succeed in School: A Guide for Parents of 4 to 14 Year Olds*, by Popkin, Youngs, and Healy, Active Parenting Publishers, Atlanta, Georgia, 1995. Refer to this excellent resource for more in-depth information.

Session 3: Research References

* Barber, Jacqueline, et al., *Insights and Outcomes: Assessments for Great Explorations in Math and Science,* Lawrence Hall of Science, Regents of the University of California, 1995.

Bracey, Gerald W., "Why Can't They Be Like We Were?" in *Phi Delta Kappan,* October, 1991.

Bredekamp, Sue, Rosegrant, Teresa, *Reaching Potentials: Transforming Early Childhood Curriculum and Assessment,* Volume 2, National Association for the Education of Young Children, Washington, DC, 1995.

* Cohen, Miriam, *First Grade Takes A Test,* Dell, New York, 1980.

Draney, K., Wilson, M., "Mapping Student Progress with Embedded Assessments: The Challenge of Making Evaluation Meaningful," Paper presented at National Evaluation Institute Workshop, Indianapolis, July, 1997.

Duschl, R.A., Gitomer, D.H., "Strategies and Challenges to Changing the Focus of Assessment and Instruction in Science Classrooms," *Educational Assessment,* 4(1), 37–73, 1997.

* Fiske, Edward B., *Smart Schools, Smart Kids: Why Do Some Schools Work?* Simon & Shuster, New York, 1992.

Gilbert, Sara, *How to Take Tests*, William Morrow and Company, Inc., New York, 1983.

Gruber, Gary, *Dr. Gruber's Essential Guide to Test Taking for Kids,* William Morrow and Company, Inc., New York, 1986.

Herman, Joan, Ansbacher, Pamela, Winters, Lynn, *A Practical Guide to Alternative Assessment*, Association for Supervision and Curriculum Development, Alexandria, Virginia, 1992.

Jorgensen, M., "Assessing Habits of Mind: Performance-Based Assessment in Science and Mathematics," ERIC Clearinghouse for Science, Mathematics, and Environmental Education, Columbus, Ohio, 1993.

Kulm, Gerald, Malcolm, Shirley (eds), *Science Assessment in the Service of Reform*, American Association for the Advancement of Science, Waldorf, Maryland, 1991.

Linn, R.L., Baker, E.L., Dunbar, S.B., "Complex, Performance-Based Assessment: Expectations and Validation Criteria," *Educational Researcher,* 20(8), 15–21, 1991.

* National Research Council/National Academy of Sciences, *National Science Education Standards*, National Academy Press, Washington, DC, 1996.

Oakes, J., Ormsmeth, T., Bell, R., Camp, P., *Multiplying Inequalities: The Effect of Race, Social Class, and Tracking on Students' Opportunities to Learn Mathematics and Science*, RAND Corporation, Santa Barbara, California, 1990.

Olson, Steve, "Science Friction" in *Education Week*, Sept. 30, 1998.

Perrone, Victor, *Expanding Student Assessment*, Association for Supervision and Curriculum Development, Alexandria, Virginia, 1991.

Pierce, Lorraine Valdez, O'Malley, Michael J., *Performance and Portfolio Assessment for Language Minority Students*, National Clearinghouse for Bilingual Education, Washington, DC, 1992.

* Popkin, Michael H., Youngs, Bettie B., Healy, Jane M., *Helping Your Child Succeed in School: A Guide for Parents of 4 to 14 Year Olds*, Active Parenting Publishers, Atlanta, Georgia, 1995.

Pursuing Excellence: A Study of U.S. Eighth-Grade Mathematics and Science Teaching, Learning, Curriculum, and Achievement in International Context, (1996); *A Study of U.S. Fourth-Grade Mathematics and Science Achievement in International Context* (1997); *A Study of U.S. Twelfth-Grade Mathematics and Science Achievement in International Context* (1998). These three reports summarize findings from TIMSS (Third International Math and Science Study) an ongoing study of student achievement with international comparisons.

Raizen, S.C., et al., *Assessment in Elementary School Science Education* and *Assessment in Science Education: The Middle Years*, National Center for Improving Science Education, Washington, DC, 1989, 1990.

Resnick, L., Resnick, D., "Assessing the Thinking Curriculum: New Tools for Educational Reform," in *Changing Assessments: Alternative Views of Aptitude, Achievement, and Instruction* (B. Gifford and M.C. O'Connor, eds.), Kluwer Academic Publishers, Boston, 1992.

Resnick, Lauren B., "Working, Thinking, and Assessment," Restructuring Learning, Council of Chief State School Officers, 1990 Summer Institute Papers and Recommendations, Washington, DC, 1993.

* The Sandia Report: Carson, C. C., Huelskamp, R. M., Woodall, T. D., "Perspectives on Education in America," in *The Journal of Educational Research*, 86(5), May/June, 1993.

Shavelson, R.J., "Performance Assessment in Science," *Applied Measurement in Education*, 4(4), 347–362, 1991.

Shymansky, J.A., et al., "The Effects of New Science Curricula on Student Performance," *Journal of Research in Science Teaching*, 20, 387–404, 1983, and "A Reassessment of the Effects of Inquiry-Based Science Curricula of the 60s," *Journal of Research in Science Teaching*, 27(2), 127–144, 1990.

* Stenmark, Jean, *Assessment Alternatives in Mathematics*, Lawrence Hall of Science, EQUALS Program, Regents of the University of California, 1989.

Stenmark, Jean, *Mathematics Assessment: Myths, Models, Good Questions, and Practical Suggestions*, National Council of Teachers of Mathematics, Reston, Virginia, 1991.

TIMSS: A Video Report. Summarizes TIMSS findings on U.S. eighth-grade education with implications for U.S. schools. 13 minutes, 1997.

Wiggins, Grant, "A True Test: Toward More Authentic and Equitable Assessment," *Phi Beta Kappan*, 703–713, May, 1989.

Engaging Messages—Session 3

The following short digests share research findings related to the information presented in Session 3: Testing: Knowing What Your Child Knows. These are best used *after* Session 3 has been presented. Some schools put one engaging message in each weekly bulletin. Parents come to expect and look forward to learning something about what research studies have found on an ongoing basis. Other schools promote attendance at future sessions by sharing some of what was learned at the previous session. Even if you don't present Session 3, these engaging messages can be used.

Educational Jargon Defined

School reform: A generic term encompassing all kinds of efforts that are taking place to improve schools. Reform efforts focus on all aspects of schooling, from how schools are governed to what curriculum is taught in the classroom.

Curriculum: The subject matter that a teacher presents to students.

Instruction: The ways in which a teacher teaches in the classroom.

Assessment: All of the many different ways (such as a written test, a portfolio of student work, an experiment, or teacher observation) that seek to measure a student's skills or knowledge in a subject area. Assessment can be both formal (students know it is a test) or informal (providing ongoing information to the teacher).

Performance-based assessment: Assessment tasks that require students to perform hands-on tasks, such as writing an essay or conducting a science experiment. Such assessments are becoming increasingly common as alternatives to multiple-choice, machine-scored tests. This is also known as authentic assessment.

Alternative assessment: Any form of measuring what students know and are able to do, other than traditional standardized tests. Alternative forms of assessment include portfolios, performance-based assessments, and other means of testing students.

Standardized tests: These are general achievement tests designed to measure how well a student has learned basic knowledge and skills taught in schools, in such areas as reading and mathematics. Popular standardized tests include: the Iowa Test of Basic Skills (ITBS), the Comprehensive Tests of Basic Skills (CTBS) and the Stanford Achievement Test Series (SAT-8, SAT-9, etc.—the number refers to which test it is in the series).

IQ test: IQ is shorthand for "intelligence quotient," which is considered to be a person's mental capacity. IQ tests have become increasingly controversial because critics claim they measure only a narrow band of intellectual strengths, primarily "school smarts." Others claim the tests are biased against members of some minority groups or are problematic in other ways.

Norm-referenced scoring: When tests are scored by comparing one student's work with other students' work.

Criterion-reference scoring: When tests are scored by comparing students' work with specific criteria or standards.

Rubric: A scoring guide for a test or other assessment task.

Standards: "Content" standards are subject-matter benchmarks designed to guide what students learn and when they should learn it. Most agree that the academic standards of public schools need to be raised—however, there is national debate over how to implement such standards—how prescriptive they should be, and whether they should be national or local, voluntary or mandated.

Standards-based reform: When standards drive reform at a school. For instance, when a school's assessment, curriculum and instruction are aligned with standards.

Helping Your Child Establish High Standards for their Schoolwork

There is lots of research evidence showing that students who know the standards for good work themselves are best able to produce good work. Asking questions like the following can help a child begin to learn these standards. Then, when your children are working on other tasks, they may ask themselves the same kind of questions.

- Explain how you figured that problem out.
- How do you know that is correct?
- Why do you think that? Write your thinking down.
- Can both of these things be true?
- Can you find a better way to convince the reader of your answer?
- Can you make a drawing that shows what you mean?
- Have you labeled your drawing?
- Did you describe the units correctly? (inches, milliliters, meters, teaspoons, etc.)
- How is this similar to what you did in class?
- What part is hard for you? How could we make that part easier?
- If a child has an incorrect solution, suggest two or three other solutions and ask them to compare them. Does one look more correct than the others?

Test results in the news

The results of standardized testing and international comparisons always seem to attract attention—especially when they are shocking! Reporters often look for attention-grabbing angles so that is how this news is typically framed. It is not uncommon for news reports to make use of simplistic interpretations of data or lump different kinds of data together to draw unwarranted conclusions. For instance, an international examination tested students for their knowledge of algebra a year before U.S. students typically study algebra in school. It's not surprising that U.S. students did not test well in algebra! Another recent report about statewide standardized test results spoke alarmingly about students' lack of knowledge as reflected by below-average test scores. Nowhere did it mention that students had 20 minutes to answer 60 questions. Rapid recall and knowledge are not the same, especially for students who are not practiced in test-taking strategy.

Bring a critical sense to what you read in the newspapers.
When reading about test results, wonder the following:

- What was the test designed to measure? Factual recall? Complex thinking?
- Were students being tested on what they were taught?
- Was there a connection between what was tested and what state or national standards say is important that students should know?
- Were students tested in a language they understood?
- Was the test measuring rapid recall or thoughtful response?
- How does what was tested relate to desired work force skills?